INSIGHT POCKET GUIDE

New E

C000071094

CHANNEL

APA PUBLICATIONS
Part of the Langenscheidt Publishing Group

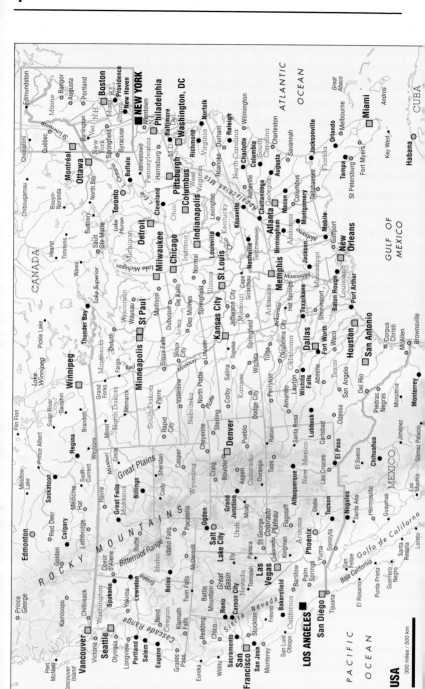

USA

300 miles / 500 km

introduction

Welcome

This guidebook combines the interests and enthusiasms of two of the world's best-known information providers: Insight Guides, who have set the standard for visual travel guides since 1970, and Discovery Channel, the world's premier source of non-fiction television programming. Its aim is to bring you the best of New England in a series of itineraries devised by two of Insight's correspondents in the region, Bill and Kay Scheller.

Comprising Maine, New Hampshire, Vermont, Massachusetts, Rhode Island and Connecticut, New England is a vast region. The 11 tours contained in this guide are therefore of between one and five days' duration and, with the exception of the city-based tours of Boston and Cambridge, they all require private transportation (information on car rental can be found in Practical Information, *page 85*). The tours begin with a three-day exploration of Boston and Cambridge, Massachusetts (with side trips to Lexington and Concord, and Lowell), and then head north for a two or three-day drive along the coast into New Hampshire (Itinerary 2), and south to Cape Cod (3). From here, the tours move clockwise southwest to Rhode Island and Narragansett Bay (4) and Connecticut's coast (5), and then inland to the Berkshire Hills (6), Vermont (7 and 8), and the Lake Winnipesaukee region and the White Mountains of New Hampshire (9 and 10). The itineraries end with a detailed exploration of the rugged Maine Coast north of Portland (11).

Supporting the itineraries are sections on history and culture, shopping, eating out, festivals, nightlife and a detailed practical information section.

Bill and Kay Scheller are a husband-and-wife travel writing team who have collaborated on 12 travel guides and are frequent contributors to national and regional US travel publications. Long-time residents of New England, the Schellers live in northern Vermont with their teenage son. They have contributed to *Insight Guide: New York State* and are the authors of guides on drives in Vermont and New Hampshire.

History and Culture

From the arrival of the first Pilgrims in 1620, through the Salem witch trials and the Revolution, to the mass tourism and high-tech developments that transformed the region in the 20th century: a look at the forces that have shaped the New England area **11**

Itineraries

contents　　7

Pages 2/3: Mount Desert Island, Maine
Pages 8/9: Acorn Street, Beacon Hill, Boston

History & Culture

New England is the home of the oldest American archetypes: the white church steeple presiding over a tidy village green; the self-sufficient farmstead; the swimming hole beneath a covered bridge; the salt-sprayed fishing village tucked against a rock-bound coast. Before the artistry of Currier & Ives in the 19th century and Norman Rockwell in the 20th century introduced these images to people who had never set foot in the region, they were everyday features in New England. And, modern, high-tech agricultural techniques notwithstanding, they still exist today.

Almost 100 years ago the writer Bernard DeVoto arrived at the conclusion that 'New England is a finished place.' But he was wrong; it remains a work in progress, and its people have grown adept at accepting – or becoming resigned to – the changes wrought by the march of time. The conservative nature of the local people is well illustrated by a popular joke: how many Vermonters does it take to screw in a light bulb? Six: one to do the job and five to harp on about how nice the old one was.

Visited by Vikings

New England's native peoples, members of the Algonkian linguistic group, were hunters and farmers. They were among the first American Indians to encounter Europeans, probably about 1,000 years ago when, it seems almost certain, Leif Ericson and his Viking followers visited New England from their base at Vinland (in what is now Canada). In the 15th or 16th century, about 100 years before England colonized the region, European fishermen set up stations along the New England coast to dry their catches of cod.

The year 2002 marks the 400th anniversary of the European discovery of Cape Cod and the island of Martha's Vineyard by England's Captain Bartholomew Gosnold. The French, too, were early explorers of the New England coast: Samuel de Champlain, sailing from Nova Scotia, ventured past the Cape and Martha's Vineyard in the first decade of the 17th century.

But as all American schoolchildren learn, the modern history of New England begins with the 1620 arrival at Plymouth of the Pilgrims, on their ship the *Mayflower*. They survived their initial bitter winter to found the first of two colonies established by English religious dissidents in an area that would take the name of a local Indian tribe, the Massachusetts. The second, a more ambitious affair founded in 1630 by the Puritan passengers of the *Arabella* was atop a hilly peninsula where the Mystic and the Charles rivers empty into an island-strewn harbor.

'We shall be as a city upon a hill,' said the

Left: Captain Parker at Lexington Battle Green
Right: portrait of a native New Englander, 1876

migrants' leader, John Winthrop, in reference to the physical aspect of creating a town and to the moral and religious paradigm that the Massachusetts Bay colony could set. The Puritans built Boston alongside the harbor.

Beginning with their Massachusetts beachheads, the newcomers labored through the 17th and 18th centuries to create the foundations of New England. Along the coast, towns such as Gloucester, Salem, and Newburyport rose to meet the needs of the fishing and shipbuilding industries, and of various trades. In the interior, the forest gave way to villages and farms. The first English settlements in New Hampshire went up in 1623, with the city of Portsmouth soon becoming a major seaport. A decade later, settlers from the Plymouth and Massachusetts Bay colonies ventured south and west to establish the first permanent towns in Connecticut. Rhode Island grew from the Providence plantations established in 1636 by Roger Williams, a clergyman disillusioned with Massachusetts Bay's theocratic government.

An early believer in the separation of church and state, Williams was in a small minority; religion and civic society were virtually indistinguishable in New England's formative years. At their worst, the Puritans hanged Quakers on Boston Common; in a more enlightened vein, they emphasized the importance of education, thereby shaping the future of a region that today enjoys its status as a center of higher learning. But in those days learning was meant to be a servant of religion: Harvard College, founded in 1636, was established to produce learned Puritan clerics and theologians; the first volume printed in New England, in 1640, was the *Bay Psalm Book*.

Salem's Witch Trials

The most ironic example of religious excess on the part of a people who had left their native land to *avoid* persecution was the Salem witch trials of 1692. In a brief season of hysteria, 20 men and women were executed for witchcraft. The trials have since been analyzed in terms ranging from class conflict to the psychology of mass delusion, but at their heart were grim notions of competing allegiances, to the divine or the diabolical, that appealed

Above: the trial of George Jacobs during Salem's period of Puritan hysteria

to the Puritan mind. The local people generally recoiled from the hysteria, and an important step in the secularization of New England was taken.

In one of the opening volleys of the racial and cultural warfare that would sear America for the next 200 years, the ascendancy of the English settlers over the native population was confirmed, once and for all, by King Philip's War (1675–76). The war, which pitted the colonists against Wampanoag and Narragansett Indians led by Chief Metacomet (also known as King Philip), ended with the defeat of the Indians at a battle on Rhode Island.

Early New England's greatest political and military challenges revolved round its relationship with the mother country, and with the threat posed by the presence of France's North American colonies to the north. New England's colonies had developed separately, and had been granted individual royal charters that were revoked in 1685 by King Charles II, who proposed that the region be ruled by a single royal governor. It was only after the deposition of his successor, James II, in 1688 that the charters were restored.

Colonial Competition

The French were a perpetual thorn in New England's side. In 1704, raiders from French Canada and their Indian allies descended on the western Massachusetts town of Deerfield, where they massacred many of the inhabitants and carried more than 100 off to captivity in Quebec. Antagonism between the colonial powers dissuaded potential settlers from moving to New England's northern frontiers. The first permanent outpost in Vermont, not far from present-day Brattleboro, was not established until 1724. The French and Indian War, in which Indian tribes fought alongside both the French and the English, ended the threat from the north. After the capitulation of the French at Quebec in 1759 and the formal transfer of jurisdiction to Britain four years later, New France ceased to exist.

By the final third of the 18th century, New England had come a long way from the hand-to-mouth existence of its early days. In the coastal cities, the income from shipping ventures created a privileged class with a taste for Georgian architecture, English luxuries, and the works of local artisans, whose exquisite furniture and silver are among the finest ever produced. These craftsmen, and the merchants and tradesmen of the cities and towns, came to constitute a new middle class.

Many small farms were built in the country-side – New England's soil, climate, and terrain were unsuited to plantation agriculture. Slavery did exist in colonial New England, primarily on a household scale among the wealthy, and some local fortunes were built on the slave trade. But the abolition of slavery was becoming a matter of religious and moral conviction in many quarters, and Vermont became the first state to outlaw the practice. Moreover, prior to the Civil War, New England was at the center of the American abolitionist movement.

Right: a tarred-and-feathered customs officer, 1770s

New England played a pivotal role in the events that presaged the American Revolution. In 1770 a local mob taunted and threw snowballs at British troops, who responded with a volley of fire that left five citizens dead. The incident became known as the Boston Massacre. Three years later the Boston Tea Party saw rebellious townsmen throwing chests of tea into the harbor to protest import duties. War broke out in Massachusetts on April 19 1775 with the battles of Lexington and Concord; two months later, the Battle of Bunker Hill was fought on the outskirts of Boston. In May of that year, the Vermont military leader Ethan Allen seized Fort Ticonderoga on Lake Champlain. In 1776, General George Washington mounted cannon captured from Ticonderoga on Dorchester Heights above Boston, forcing the British from the city. For the remainder of the war, which ended in 1783, the action shifted almost entirely to the middle and southern colonies.

The end of the Revolution marked the beginning of a golden age of New England trade. This was the era in which merchants sent their ships to east Asian ports to collect cargoes of tea, silks, porcelain, and other exotic goods in what became known as the China Trade. The era's legacy is preserved in the old seaport cities' elegant Federalist-style mansions, particularly in Salem, Newburyport, and Portsmouth. A depression in maritime trade began in 1807 when President Thomas Jefferson placed an embargo on commerce with France and Britain in retaliation for interference by those nations with American shipping. The downturn was exacerbated by the 1812–14 war with Britain. Trade resumed in the course of the following decades, which also comprised the glory years of New England's whaling fleet.

Vermont and Maine Join the USA

The end of the 18th century ushered in an era of prosperity for the region's farmers, who cleared the woodlands of the northern and western frontiers for agriculture. Vermont joined the United States in 1791, Maine in 1820. It has been said that, except for salt and nails, the upcountry New England farms of the early 19th century were self-sufficient. In addition to providing for themselves and the villages that served as their market centers, northern New England farmers raised beef cattle that were driven to Boston, and developed a sheep industry that, 200 years later, is undergoing a revival.

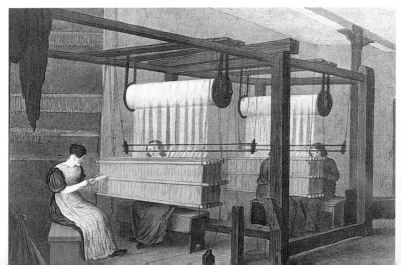

Logging was the other great 19th-century enterprise in the north country. Trees were felled in forest lumber camps in Maine, New Hampshire, and Vermont, and river drives saw huge amounts of timber float downstream to the mills. Logging held sway in rural New England until, later in the century, the bigger country of the upper Midwest came into its own.

By the 1830s the profits from the China Trade were financing America's Industrial Revolution. Led by visionary capitalists such as Nathan Appleton, and fired with enthusiasm for the mechanized textile-weaving technology demonstrated by Samuel Slater in 1793 at his cotton mill in Pawtucket, Rhode Island, New England entrepreneurs got busy. The most ambitious projects focused on the Merrimack River, with Manchester in New Hampshire, and Lawrence and Lowell in Massachusetts, becoming the region's most important textile cities. The production of shoes, tools, clocks, firearms, and numerous other items led to New England's claim to be America's workshop.

The growth of industry added a new cultural dimension to New England. Staffed at first by native hands – in some cases, by farm girls who lived in company dormitories – the mills developed an appetite for labor that the local population could not satisfy. Manufacturers recruited workers in rural Quebec, and by the late 19th century Canadian French was a second language in many mill towns. Continental European and Irish immigrants poured into the factories, bringing a cosmopolitan flavor to a corner of America that had remained stoutly Anglo-Saxon for generations.

A Literary Tradition

While industry was transforming the region's landscape, a coterie of writers centered in Boston and Concord created the first important movement in American literature. In 1836, Ralph Waldo Emerson published his essay *Nature*, which marked the genesis of Transcendentalism, a philosophy stressing the unity of personal spirituality with the divinity inherent in all things. In the following years Emerson's neighbor, Henry David Thoreau, chronicled his relationship with the natural world and his sojourn in a hand-built cabin on the shores of Walden Pond.

Another sometime Concord man, Nathaniel Hawthorne, brought a psychological dimension to the American novel. And he cast a sharp eye on Puritan New England in *The Scarlet Letter*. Hawthorne's friend Herman Melville spent his most productive years in New England. He used his knowledge of the New Bedford whaling industry as background for *Moby Dick*, completed in 1851. Adding luster to New England's literary reputation in the mid-19th century were Louisa May Alcott, Henry Wadsworth Longfellow, and John Greenleaf Whittier.

The abolitionist spirit of New Englanders such as Whittier and the fervent Massachusetts orator William Lloyd Garrison inspired thousands of men to leave the region's cities, towns, and farms for the battlefields of the Civil War. New England industries benefited enormously from the war, and from the ensuing boom years. Throughout the Gilded Age (the term was coined as

Left: new textile machinery was introduced in the early 19th century
Right: Nathaniel Hawthorne, 1804–1864, novelist and man of letters

the title for a novel co-authored by Charles Dudley Warner and an adopted New Englander, Mark Twain), New England remained an industrial dynamo. The textile industry, the region's premier creator of profits and jobs, reached the apex of its prosperity at the beginning of the 20th century.

As the new century dawned, New England grew into its role as custodian of much of the nation's past, as the standard-bearer of a society that looked backward rather than forward. This realm was chronicled, in both fiction (John P. Marquand's *The Late George Apley*) and nonfiction (Cleveland Amory's *The Proper Bostonians*), as a world in which most of what mattered had already happened. The cultural environment in places such as Boston became genteel and staid. Upcountry, the melancholy aspect of hardscrabble farms lent a somber atmosphere to the poems of Robert Frost; it was not an environment in which it was easy to put food on the table.

Tourism and High Tech

During the latter half of the 20th century, two phenomena served to reverse the decline of New England and change its relationship with the rest of the country. The first, tourism, benefited from the discovery that a landscape intrinsically varied and beautiful, and overlaid with a rich human history, could attract a substantial number of visitors. In the 19th century, palatial hotels along the seashore and at various points in the New Hampshire mountains catered to a wealthy clientele. But after World War II, tourism in New England became diffused and democratized, especially when entrepreneurs began stringing rope tows, and later chair lifts, along the sides of mountains that were destined to become ski resorts.

The second phenomenon was the explosion of the high-tech and financial-services sectors, a direct outgrowth of New England's long tradition of investment in higher education. In addition to the colleges and universities themselves, these growing industries brought new life and new ideas not only to the big cities and established suburbs, but also to smaller cities and towns: the computer revolution encouraged decentralization. Today, it's not unusual to see high-tech firms ensconced in once-abandoned textile mills, or to encounter people who run sophisticated businesses out of remote rural addresses.

New England has always traded in intellectual ideas as well as material merchandise. The steady influx of new-comers – of tourists who decided to stay, students who remained after taking their degrees, and people lured by the new business atmosphere – has made the region an exciting laboratory for new ideas in areas ranging from land use and environmental policy to financing public education and promoting alternative energy sources. The entire region is, one might argue, a city upon a hill.

Left: fishing has come a long way

HISTORY HIGHLIGHTS

1602 English explorer Captain Bartholomew Gosnold sights Cape Cod and Martha's Vineyard.

1620 *Mayflower* Pilgrims arrive at Plymouth.

1623 First English settlements in New Hampshire.

1630 Puritan settlers establish Boston and Massachusetts Bay Company.

1633–36 First English settlements in Connecticut (chartered 1662).

1636 Harvard College, the nation's first institution of higher learning, founded at Cambridge, Massachusetts.

1636 Religious dissident Roger Williams founds Rhode Island colony (chartered 1663).

1675–76 King Philip's War pits Wampanoag and Narragansett Indians against colonists.

1692 Twenty people are executed for witchcraft at Salem, Massachusetts.

1704 French and allied Indians stage Deerfield Raid, attacking western Massachusetts town, killing many settlers and taking captives to Canada.

1724 First permanent European settlement in Vermont.

1754–63 French and Indian War, fought with New England participation on British side, ends France's American empire.

1765 Stamp Act, mandating tax stamps on documents, stirs anti-British feeling.

1770 British soldiers fire upon mob, killing five in 'Boston Massacre.'

1775 American Revolution begins with battles of Lexington and Concord. The Battle of Bunker Hill follows in June.

1776 British routed from Boston.

1783 American Revolution ends.

1791 Vermont becomes 14th state.

1793 Samuel Slater introduces mechanized textile manufacturing to New England at Pawtucket, Rhode Island.

1807–14 New England shipping suffers as a result of an embargo set by President Jefferson.

1812–14 War with Britain.

1820 Maine, which was a part of Massachusetts, becomes a state.

1822 The Merrimack Manufacturing Company is founded at Lowell, Massachusetts; it becomes harbinger of the region's industrial prowess.

1830–36 First New England railroads link Boston with outlying cities.

1845–50 Boston is the destination of thousands fleeing Ireland's potato famine; the newcomers herald a radical change in the city's ethnic composition.

1861–65 Staunchly abolitionist New England sends troops to fight in the Civil War; Vermont suffers the highest casualty rate in the Union.

c1900 Amoskeag Mills in Manchester, New Hampshire, constitute the largest textile producer in the world.

1921 Italian anarchists Nicola Sacco and Bartolomeo Vanzetti arrested for payroll robbery and murder; the case polarizes the radical movement. The two are executed in 1927.

1934 Advent of the first mechanical ski tow in Vermont; huge regional industry develops after World War II.

1935 Amoskeag mills close, as textile industry moves south.

1960 Bostonian John F. Kennedy is elected president; he establishes Cape Cod National Seashore to preserve undeveloped Cape lands.

1960s High-tech industry burgeons along Massachusetts' Route 128, thereby transforming the region's economic complexion.

1990s Severe limitations are imposed on cod fishery in response to dwindling stocks; numerous traditional livelihoods are threatened.

1990s Controversy over disposition of paper-company lands in Vermont, New Hampshire, and Maine; future of vast forest tracts at stake.

2000 Edward Kennedy re-elected as Massachusetts senator.

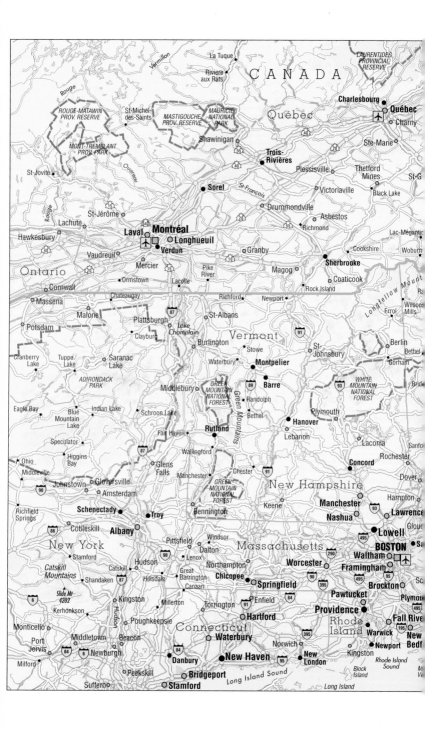

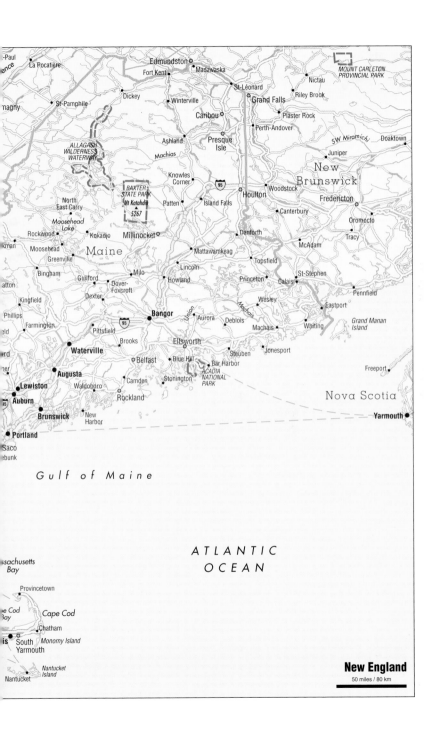

-Paul
ence
La Pocatière
St-Pamphile
nagny

Edmundston
Fort Kent
Madawaska
St-Léonard
Nictau
Riley Brook
Grand Falls
Dickey
Winterville
Caribou
Plaster Rock
Perth-Andover

MOUNT CARLETON
PROVINCIAL PARK

SW Miramichi
Doakton

ALLAGASH
WILDERNESS
WATERWAY
Ashland
Presque
Isle
Machias
Juniper

New
Brunswick

North
East Carry
BAXTER
STATE PARK
Mt Katahdin
5267
Knowles
Corner
95
Patten
Island Falls
Woodstock
Houlton
Fredericton

Moosehead
Lake
Rockwood
Kokadjo
Millinocket
Danforth
Canterbury
Oromocto
Tracy

kman
Moosehead
Greenville
Maine
Mattawamkeag
Topsfield
McAdam

Bingham
Guilford
Dover-
Foxcroft
Milo
Lincoln
Howland
Princeton
Calais
St-Stephen

Kingfield
Dexter
Wesley
Pennfield

Phillips
Farmington
Pittsfield
Union
Bangor
Aurora
Deblois
Machias
Machais
Whiting
Eastport

Grand Manan
Island

eld
rd
ner

Waterville
Brooks
Ellsworth
Steuben
Jonesport

Augusta
Belfast
Blue Hill
Bar Harbor
Freeport

Lewiston
Camden
Stonington
ACADIA
NATIONAL
PARK

Auburn
95
Waldoboro
Rockland

Nova Scotia

Brunswick
New
Harbor

Portland
Saco
ebunk

Yarmouth

Gulf of Maine

*ATLANTIC
OCEAN*

sachusetts
Bay

Provincetown

e Cod
Bay
Cape Cod
Chatham

is
South
Yarmouth
Monomy Island

*Nantucket
Island*
Nantucket

New England
50 miles / 80 km

New England
Itineraries

1. BOSTON AND CAMBRIDGE,
MASSACHUSETTS *(see maps, p22, 26–7 & 29)*

Boston and Cambridge are easily explored on foot but there is a lot to
see so allow at least three days for these cities. Having seen the major
urban sites, head west to the towns that initiated the American Revolution,
and to Lowell, a cradle of the Industrial Revolution. Allow a day for
Lexington/Concord and a day for Lowell.

*From Boston, drive to Lexington and Concord on Route 2A; return on Route 2.
Lowell is northwest of Boston at the intersection of Route 3 and I-495.*

No American city is as dense with historical and cultural landmarks as
Boston. And few if any possess as complex an overlay of places and things
relating to so many different eras: in its compact central quarter, Boston
condenses nearly 400 years of history.

Fortunately for visitors with limited time, Boston's **Freedom Trail** links
all of the major sites associated with colonial and Revolutionary history.
Get oriented at the **Boston National Historical Park Visitors Center** (Old
State House, 15 State Street; daily 9am–5pm; tel: 617-242 5642; guided
tours available); or at the **Visitors Information Center** on Boston Common (Tremont near West Street; daily 9am–5pm; tel: 617-536 4100). The
Trail includes 16 sites, all within a 2½-mile (4km) walk. Downtown sites
include the 1713 **Old State House** (206 Washington Street; daily 9am–5pm;
tel: 617-720 3290). This, the former seat of Britain's colonial government,
now houses a museum of Revolutionary history. Also interesting is the **Old
South Meeting House** (310 Washington Street; tel: 617-482 6439), where
Revolutionary activity included Samuel Adams's exhortations before the celebrated Boston Tea Party of 1773. (You can see a replica of the Tea Party ship
Beaver, which is moored at the Congress Street Bridge; tel: 617-338 1773.)

Faneuil Hall and Quincy Market

From the Old State House, follow State Street toward the waterfront
to reach the handsome Georgian **Faneuil Hall** (Faneuil Hall Square;
daily 9am–5am), built in 1742 and frequently the site of protest meet-
ings in pre-Revolutionary Boston. Opposite are the
granite arcades of **Quincy Market**, built in 1826
as a public marketplace and renovated in the 1970s.
Today a festive gallimaufry of stores, restaurants,
cafés, and food stalls, Quincy Market is the perfect
place to grab coffee or a snack before pressing on to
Boston's oldest part – the North End.

The Freedom Trail continues along the narrow
streets of the North End, renowned in recent years

Left: sailboats on Boston's Charles River
Right: sculpture on the Old State House

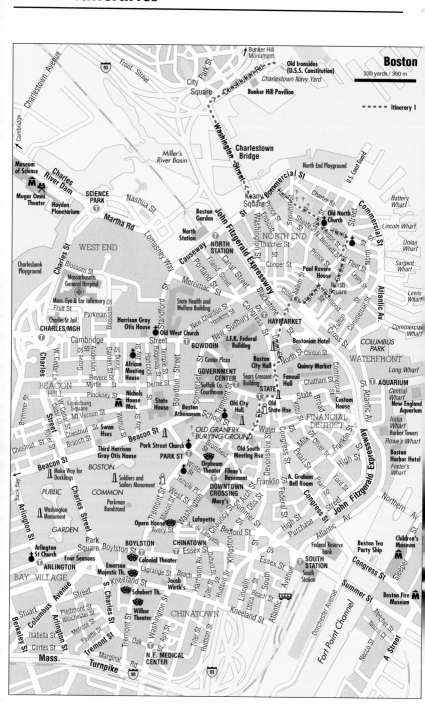

Boston

330 yards / 300 m

••••• Itinerary 1

as a predominantly Italian neighborhood but originally, before the city was expanded by landfill projects, the center of colonial Boston. Here you will find the city's oldest surviving residence, the **Paul Revere House** (19 North Square; tel: 617-523 2338). The *circa*-1670s residence is where Revere was living when he took his famous ride on the night of April 18, 1775. His dash into the countryside to warn other Patriots of British troop movements was preceded by a lantern signal from the steeple of **Old North Church** (193 Salem Street; daily 9am–5pm; tel: 617-523 6676), the oldest house of worship in Boston. Still in use, it was based on designs by Christopher Wren and has an exquisite interior. On Salem and surrounding streets there are plenty of places at which to relax with an espresso and Italian pastry.

Old Ironsides

Stroll across the Charlestown Bridge from the North End to visit two outlying Freedom Trail sites, both in the Charlestown neighborhood on the far side of the Charles River. The USS *Constitution* (Charlestown Navy Yard, off Water Street; tel: 617-426 1812), known as 'Old Ironsides', was built in Boston in 1797. The US Navy's oldest commissioned warship, it emerged victorious from 42 engagements in the early 19th century. Navy personnel give tours of the vessel, and a related museum is adjacent to her berth. A few blocks away, the **Bunker Hill Monument** (Monument Street; daily 9am–4.30pm; tel: 617-242 5641) is a severe granite shaft erected in 1843 to commemorate the June 17, 1775 Battle of Bunker Hill. A climb of nearly 300 steps leads to terrific harbor views.

The **Museum of Science** (Science Park; tel: 617-723 2500) is linked to downtown via the

Above: at the New England Aquarium
Right: the USS *Constitution*, aka 'Old Ironsides'

Charles River Dam bridge. The museum's wealth of detailed exhibits – many of them interactive – offer lively explanations of scientific principles and technology. There is a planetarium and an Omni theater on the premises. Central Boston's other big draw for children is the **New England Aquarium** (Central Wharf; open daily; tel: 617-973 5200), with many of its 2,000 species live in a four-story central cylindrical tank.

Many visitors think of Boston as a genteel old city built with warm red bricks, where gaslamps glow in the evening on streets bordered by stately townhouses. This is the Boston of **Beacon Hill**, the compact neighborhood between Beacon, Charles, Cambridge, and Bowdoin streets. Facing Boston Common (the oldest public park in the nation) at the hill's crest is the 1795 **Massachusetts State House** (tours Mon–Sat 10am–4pm; tel 617-727 3676), built to a masterful design by Charles Bulfinch. Graced by a gilded dome that seems to float above its late-Georgian facade, the State House has legislative chambers, a governor's office, and a hall of Massachusetts battle flags.

Paul Revere's Resting Place

Follow Park Street from Beacon directly in front of the State House, and you will reach the **Granary Burying Ground**, next to Park Street Church, where Paul Revere and other patriots are buried. Follow Beacon Street away from the hill, toward downtown, to arrive at **King's Chapel**, where gravestones date to the 17th century.

The streets of Beacon Hill are lined with some of the finest residential architecture in the US. Particularly notable are Louisburg Square, which surrounds an exquisite private park, and Mt Vernon and Chestnut streets, where more of Bulfinch's graceful architecture is on display. Charles Street, at the base of the hill, with its antique dealers and specialty stores, bars, and cafes, is ideal for browsing.

Above: capturing the light in the Public Garden
Left: headstone in the King's Chapel cemetery

Cross Beacon Street at Charles Street to enter the **Public Garden**, a formal park whose pedal-powered **swan boats** take passengers for leisurely cruises amid the ducks on a pretty little 'lagoon.' The Garden marks the beginning of the 19th-century landfill neighborhood called **Back Bay**, where broad boulevards are lined with Victorian townhouses. Though primarily residential, Back Bay has two of Boston's most renowned shopping thoroughfares: chic **Newbury Street**, lined with upscale boutiques, and **Boylston Street**, which leads to the **Prudential Center** and **Copley Place** shopping malls.

Copley Square, at the heart of Back Bay, is home to two of the city's finest architectural feats. **Trinity Church**, the 1877 Romanesque masterwork by Henry Hobson Richardson, has a rough-hewn polychrome exterior and lush interior paintings and glass by Oliver LaForge, William Morris, and Edward Burne-Jones. Facing the church across the square is the **Boston Public Library**, built in 1895 to a Renaissance revival design by McKim, Mead, and White. The ornate interior has murals by Edwin Abbey and Pierre Puvis de Chavannes. Between the two buildings stands an elegant hotel, the 1912 **Fairmont Copley Plaza** (138 St James Avenue; tel: 617-267 5300).

Continue down Boylston Street for seven blocks to the Fenway. Less than a mile down the Fenway, to your left, are Boston's two finest art museums. The larger, the **Museum of Fine Arts** (465 Huntington Avenue; daily, Wed till 9.45pm, tel: 617-267 9300), exhibits an astounding array of fine and decorative American art, and a French Impressionist collection that includes 38 Monets. The museum is also strong on Egyptian and Asian antiquities. A block away, the **Isabella Stewart Gardner Museum** (289 The Fenway; tel: 617-566 1401) stands as a monument to one art aficionado's quirkiness and exquisite taste. Mrs Gardner built this replica of a Venetian palazzo in 1903 as her own home, and to househer collections of European masters (including the likes of Titian's *Rape of Europa*). Her will stipulated that everything in the house be left exactly as she had arranged it. Sunday concerts in the tapestry room are a special treat.

Harvard, Heart of Cambridge

Cambridge, easily accessible by subway from Boston, can also be reached by fairly ambitious walkers – a stroll along the parks that line the Boston side of the Charles River is one of the city's finest experiences. The heart of Cambridge is **Harvard Square**, ever-bustling gateway to the nation's oldest university (dating to 1636). University buildings occupy much of the land around the square. The area's many stores, coffeehouses, bars, and restaurants unfortunately no longer project the unpredictable, idiosyncratic milieu of the time before sky-high rents. Enter the university's august gates into Harvard Yard – visitors are welcome to soak up the Ivy League atmosphere and use the facilities provided by the university's excellent museums (Mon–Sat; Sun pm).

Right: statue of George Washington in the Public Garden

Of these, the **Fogg Art Museum** (32 Quincy St; tel: 617-495 9400) has a fine American and European collection that is particularly strong in medieval Italian work. The connecting **Busch-Reisinger Museum** is good for Germanic art. A few blocks away – and included in the price of an admission ticket to the Fogg – is the **Arthur M. Sackler Museum** (485 Broadway; tel: 617-495 9400). This striking postmodern structure is filled with Asian, Islamic, and Greek and Roman art.

Harvard's science collections are gathered in the **Peabody Museum of Archaeology and Ethnology** (11 Divinity Avenue; tel: 617-496 1027) and in the **Harvard Museum of Natural History** (26 Oxford Street; tel: 617-495 3045).

The Peabody houses an extensive collection of anthropological items, particularly relating to the Americas; the Museum of Natural History is divided into separate exhibitions of minerals and geology, comparative zoology, and botany. The botanical collection centers on a series of glass flowers, 3,000 models of plant species made by a father-and-son glassmaking team over the course of more than 60 years.

Side Trip to Lexington and Concord

The fire that ignited the American Revolution was famously kindled on April 19, 1775, at the Massachusetts villages of **Lexington** and **Concord**. Sites associated with the war's opening engagements (and indeed with a seminal era in American literature) are within easy reach of Boston. For Lexington, head west from the city via Routes 2 and 4/225 for 12 miles (19km). **Lexington Green** was the site of the first fighting on that fateful April morning. Guarded by the **Minuteman Statue** at its eastern entrance,

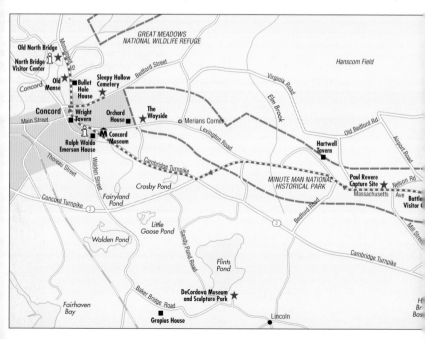

the Green is today the venue of an annual re-enactment on the battle date. Nearby you will find the 1738 **Hancock-Clarke House** (36 Hancock Street; tel: 781-861 0928), where Paul Revere warned John Hancock and Samuel Adams of the British advance, and also the 17th-century **Buckman Tavern** (1 Bedford St; tel: 781-862 5598), where wounded Minutemen were treated. The original bullet holes can still be seen in the door.

Concord, site of the second, April 19, battle, is 8 miles (13km) west of Lexington – take Route 2A, the 'Battle Road' that follows the route of the 1775 combatants. The journey passes through **Minute Man National Historical Park** (Visitors Center, Route 2A; tel: 781-862 7753). On Monument Street, just north of town, part of the national park surrounds the replica **Old North Bridge** where the battle, in which the Patriots routed British regulars, was centered. **Old North Bridge Visitors Center** (daily 9am–5pm; tel: 978-369 6993) has period artifacts and dioramas that explain the encounter.

Some 50 years after the battle, Concord had become New England's liveliest literary town. The **Old Manse** (tel: 878-369 3909) on the park grounds was at different times the home of both Hawthorne and Emerson. In Concord's village center is the **Emerson House** (28 Cambridge Turnpike; tel: 978-369 2236), where the great essayist lived for many years. **Orchard House** (399 Lexington Road; tel: 978-369 4118) was the home of Louisa May Alcott. Emerson's study and artifacts relating to Thoreau are displayed in the **Concord Museum** (200 Lexington Road; tel: 978-369 9763). Thoreau's Walden Pond is a few miles away. Alcott, Emerson, Thoreau, and Hawthorne are all buried in Concord's **Sleepy Hollow Cemetery** on Bedford Street.

Side Trip to Lowell

Lowell, 32 miles (51km) north of Boston (take I-93 north to I-95 south, then Route 3 north) cradled a revolution as dynamic in its way as the one ignited at Lexington and Concord. It was here, in 1822, that a Boston syndicate began to develop a community around a complex of water-powered textile mills on the Merrimack River. Lowell grew to become a manufacturing center, although its decline was precipitous during the 20th-century migration of textile jobs to the South.

In the 1980s the development of **Lowell National Historical Park** (Visitors Center, 46 Market Street; tel: 459 1000) helped to revitalize Lowell while adapting the old mill build-

Lexington and Concord

1750 yards / 1600 m

Above Left: John Harvard

ings as museums and centers devoted to industrial history. In addition to excellent exhibits relating to technology and immigrant labor, the park's attractions include the **Boott Mill**, where power looms still turn out cloth. (You might want to take home a freshly made cotton dish-towel as a souvenir.) This is also the place from which to take a summer barge tour around the city's canals. You might also want to join one of the interesting guided walking and trolley tours.

2. MASSACHUSETTS NORTH SHORE AND NEW HAMPSHIRE SEACOAST *(see map, p29 & 31)*

A two or three-day tour of historic towns on the Massachusetts coast north of Boston. The drive extends along the New Hampshire coast, ending at the colonial capital of Portsmouth.

Take route 1A, with a Cape Ann loop involving routes 127, 127A, and 133. Returning to Boston from Portsmouth, take I-95 south.

The North Shore of Massachusetts and the New Hampshire coastline are steeped in the maritime heritage of New England, and provide spectacular seashore scenery along with some of the region's finest architecture. The great days of fishing, shipbuilding, and trade along this coast are long past, and much of what you will see is the result of conscientious preservation. The North Shore's Gloucester wharves still smell of fish, the summer homes along Cape Ann's rugged shores still bear the patina of old money, and, in Newburyport, Market Square still looks as if it is preparing for the next clipper due to dock in the port.

On the 15-mile (24km) drive up the coast from Boston to Salem, suburban

Above: April 19, 1775 revisited
Left: an all-American symbol

and industrial stretches are punctuated by ocean views. For the best view, detour off Route 1A at Swampscott and take route 129 to **Marblehead**, a trove of 18th-century homes. Near the center of town, **Abbott Hall** (188 Washington Street; tel: 781-631 0528) houses Archibald Willard's painting *The Spirit of '76*, depicting a now-famous trio of Revolutionary warriors: drummer, fife player, and flag bearer.

The Wealth of Salem

Next up is **Salem** – take Route 114 back onto Route 1A and continue north – a seaport that once appeared to have such fabulous wealth that Asian traders thought it was a nation unto itself. There followed years of decline, then a program of restoration, the best evidence of which is along **Chestnut Street**. This 200-year-old street is considered by many urban connoisseurs to be among the country's most beautiful thoroughfares.

The **Salem Maritime National Historic Site** (174 Derby Street; daily 9am–5pm; tel: 978-740 1660) on the waterfront incorporates Derby Wharf, Custom House, and Warehouse, all rich in associations with the China Trade. Also along here is the 18th-century Derby House, which was the home of one of Salem's most prosperous merchant princes.

The **Peabody Essex Museum** (East India Square; Mon–Sat 10am–5pm, Sun pm only; tel: 978-745 9500 or 1-800 745 4054) is the other prime custodian of Salem's seafaring past. Founded to exhibit items brought home by Salem's seafarers, it has become one of the nation's premier repositories of Asian art. It is also a trove of maritime treasures, with exhibits ranging from scrimshaw (the art of decorating or carving shells, bone or ivory, which was a popular sailors' pastime) to figureheads.

Another role undertaken by the Peabody Essex is the maintenance of three historic homes, including the 1805 **Gardner-Pingree House**, considered to be Salem architect and woodcarver Samuel McIntire's masterpiece. The house is a textbook study in the restrained Federal style, characterized by a masterful use of proportion. McIntire's work represents Salem at its sunny zenith.

But it wasn't always such a tranquil place. In the 1690s, when Salem and its neighbor Danvers village were struggling outposts, the area was gripped by witch hysteria. Today there are numerous reminders of the infamous witch trials. The stark 1642 **Witch House** (310 Essex Street;

Boston to Portsmouth
15 miles / 25 km

Mar 15–Nov 30 10am–4.30pm; tel: 978-744 0180) was the home of one of the presiding judges. The **Witch Museum** (19 Washington Square North; Sept–June daily 10am–5pm; Jul–Aug 10am–7pm; tel: 978-744 1692) presents an historically accurate, if melodramatic, account of that time of mass hysteria through sound-and-light tableaus inside a dark 1840s church.

Salem's most famous landmark earned its place in history not through its role in actual events, but due to its literary connections. The *circa* 1688 **House of the Seven Gables** (54 Turner Street; daily 10am–5pm, until 7pm summer; tel: 978-744 0991) was the home of a cousin of Salem-born author Nathaniel Hawthorne, who immortalized the house in his novel of the same name. Hawthorne's birthplace, which has been moved from its original location, is also at this site. A statue of the famous author stands on downtown's Hawthorne Boulevard not far from the small, quietly elegant **Hawthorne Hotel** (18 Washington Square; tel: 978-745 9842).

Hammond Castle

At **Beverly**, on the other side of the Danvers River, pick up Route 127 and meander along the south coast of **Cape Ann**. The sight of steep, shingled gables tucked among the trees shows that there is still life in what was,

during the Gilded Age, a prime location for the summer retreats of Boston's upper classes. The most individualistic of these properties is **Hammond Castle** (Route 127; Thurs, Fri, Sat, Sun am; tel: 978-283 2080), a stone stronghold built by inventor John Hays Hammond Jr in the 1920s. Hammond made his money in electronics, but his heart was in the Middle Ages and he plundered Europe for elements to work into his dreamhouse. Along with a massive pipe organ, the place is filled with interior details acquired from real medieval castles.

Continue into **Gloucester** (16 miles/26km from Salem). This town was founded in 1623 and is Massachusetts' oldest fishing port. More recently the town starred in the 2000 film of Sebastian Junger's best-selling book *A Perfect Storm*, recounting the loss of the *Andrea Gail* fishing boat in 120-mile-an-hour winds. The spirit of the fishery – which is now threatened by the depletion of cod stocks – is beautifully captured in the form of the **Fisherman Statue** on the waterfront: a helmsman in rain gear holds fast to his wheel, above the inscription 'They Who Go Down to the Sea in Ships 1630–1930.'

The **Cape Ann Historical Association** (27 Pleasant Street; Tues–Sat 10am–5pm; tel: 978-283 0455) is situated in the sloping streets above the

Above: modern-day 'witches' in Salem
Above Right: maritime accommodations in Gloucester

harbor. This fascinating museum features ship models, furnishings, silver items, and marine paintings, including works by Gloucester-born luminist Fitz-Hugh Lane. Out amid the mansions of exclusive Eastern Point, the quirky **Beauport** (75 Eastern Point Boulevard; mid-May–mid-Oct 10am–4pm; weekends pm only; tel: 978-283 0800) represents the life's work of decorator and collector Henry Davis Sleeper. In the years between 1907 and 1934, Sleeper added room after room to his rambling home, each reflecting a different period. He would have carried on building, but when the number of rooms reached 40, the neighbors decided that enough was enough. If you are looking for accommodation, White Rainbow (65 Main Street; tel: 978-281 0017) is a longtime favorite with visitors.

Swims and Walks

After a stroll through the art galleries of **Rocky Neck**, or a swim at lovely **Wingaersheek Beach**, continue along Route 127A for 2 miles (3km) to Gloucester's upscale neighbor, **Rockport**. Downtown's cramped little lanes all seem to converge on **Bearskin Neck**, a narrow arm of land lined from beginning to end with stores and galleries. Walk out to the end of the neck for lovely views of the harbor – and of the bright red fishing shack known as Motif No 1 due to its popularity as a subject for amateur painters. Wrecked by the devasting blizzard of 1978, it was rebuilt to keep the artists coming. The Yankee Clipper Inn (96 Granite Street; tel: 978-546 3407) offers fine seaside accommodation, and you're never far from a decent bowl of clam chowder around Bearskin Neck.

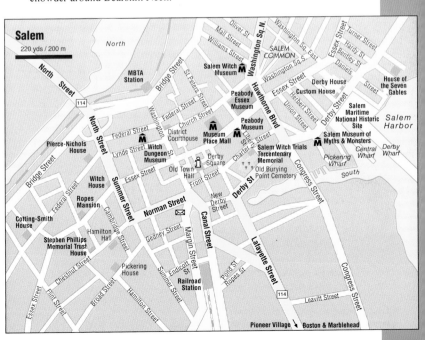

Antiques and Fried Clams

Drive around the northern tip of Cape Ann on Route 127 – this rocky coast, which once supported a granite industry, gave Rockport its name – and continue for 13 miles (21km) via Route 126 to Route 133 north and the village of **Essex**. Once a thriving shipbuilding community, Essex now sprawls quietly along miles of salt marshes. Its single main street is devoted to one of New England's greatest concentrations of antique shops, along with restaurants specializing in fried clams. The dish was allegedly invented here at **Woodman's** (Route 1A), which is still a popular stop for lovers of the sweet local bivalves.

Ipswich, 6 miles (10km) north of Essex, dates back to 1633, and is another of Massachusetts' oldest coastal settlements. Just before you get to the town center – a single intersection with a cluster of stores and taverns – look out for the 1640 **John Whipple House** (1 South Village Green; May–Oct Wed–Sat 10am–4pm, Sun 1–4pm; tel: 978-356 2811), which was home to six generations of the Whipple family. It is an unusually large and well-preserved example of a 'first period' colonial home, furnished with fine 17th-century antiques. Turn down leafy Argilla Road to reach **Crane's Beach** (tel: 978-356 4354), one of the North Shore's most popular swimming spots.

Georgian Newburyport

Continuing on Route 1A, pass through the towns of Rowley and Newbury, where in the fall you may see dome-shaped stacks of salt hay, still harvested as it was centuries ago. The stacks and surrounding tawny marshes were a favorite subject of luminist painters. The small city of **Newburyport**, 12 miles (19km) north of Ipswich, prospered from maritime trade at the beginning of the 19th century and during the clipper-ship era of the 1850s. Its decline was halted some 30 years ago by the arrival of newcomers who appreciated its preserved Georgian and Federal homes, and its compact downtown, which was harmoniously rebuilt following a fire in 1811.

For a good perspective on Newburyport history, visit the 1808 **Cushing**

Above: Rockport harbor, featuring the red fishing shack known as Motif No 1

House (98 High St; May–Oct Tues–Sat 11am–2pm; tel: 878-462 2681). This sea captain's mansion is full of period furnishings and China Trade artifacts. The collections at the **Custom House Maritime Museum** (25 Water Street; tel: 978-462 8681) are devoted to nautical themes.

Newburyport offers a selection of B&Bs, several in gracious homes that have stood for two centuries or more. If you would prefer a small hotel, try the Garrison Inn (11 Brown Square; tel: 978-499 8500). For dinner, the down-home Grog (13 Middle Street), all bricks, beams, and burgers, with live music on weekends, is recommended. Also good is the intimate, chic Scandia (25 State Street; tel: 978-462 6271).

In the morning, head out of the causeway to Plum Island and the **Parker River Wildlife Refuge**. This lovely preserve, encompassing dunes, salt marsh, and scrub woodland, is one of the east coast's best birding sites. The refuge's ocean beaches are wonderful, and limited parking facilities keeps the crowds at bay.

Hampton Beach and Portsmouth

Crossing into New Hampshire, it's a 19-mile (31km) drive from Newbury-port to Portsmouth. Although you can take the limited-access I-95, Route 1A offers a more varied if slower trip. This coast road passes through the honky-tonk heart of **Hampton Beach**. In summer this resort teems with vacation-ers attracted by the surf, pop concerts (either outdoors or at the Hampton Beach Casino), weekly fireworks displays, arcades, and bars. Farther north, there are several less rollicking places at which to take a dip or a stroll along the shore. Of these, **Odiorne Point State Park** is a good choice.

In **Portsmouth** there are still signs of the town's 18th-century heyday when, as the capital of the New Hampshire colony, it was a busy ship-building center and seaport. (The nation's oldest naval shipyard still thrives on a nearby island.) Many of Portsmouth's handsomely restored period homes are clustered in **Strawbery Banke** (Marcy Street; mid-Apr–Oct: daily 10am–5pm; tel: 603-433 1100). This neighborhood of 42 preserved houses illustrates local architecture and lifestyles ranging from the 17th century through to the 1950s.

The 1763 **Moffatt-Ladd House** (154 Market Street; mid-June–mid-Oct Mon–Sat 11am–5pm, Sun 1–5pm; tel: 603-436 8221) is rich in period details. The 1760 **Wentworth-Gardner House** (Gardner and Mechanic streets; mid-June–mid-Oct Tues–Sun 1–4pm; tel: 603-436 4406) has elaborate woodwork and hand-painted wallpapers. The **Wentworth-Coolidge Mansion** (Little Harbor Road; June–Oct Tues–Sat 10am–3pm, Sun 1–5pm; tel: 603-436 6607) was governor Benning Wentworth's residence and is still furnished with many of his belongings.

Downtown Portsmouth bustles with stores, restaurants, and cafes. Reminiscent of a 19th-century club, the Library (401 State Street; tel: 603-431 5202) is a relaxing place for dinner. If you plan to spend the night here, the Sise

Right: New England fishermen come in all sizes

Inn (40 Court St; tel: 603-433 1200) offers plush, Victorian-themed rooms in a Queen Anne mansion.

If there are still a few hours left in the day – or for an offbeat start on the following morning – take the boat cruise (315 Market Street; tel: 603-431 5500 or 1-800 441 4620) from Portsmouth harbor to the **Isles of Shoals**, a rugged little archipelago lying 10 miles (16km) offshore. The trip includes stops at Star Island, where a rambling old hotel hosts summer arts conferences, and at remote Appledore Island, where the 19th-century poet Celia Thaxter nurtured a literary salon, replete with works by American Impressionist Childe Hassam , and a lovely garden).

3. SOUTH SHORE AND CAPE COD *(see map, p36)*

A four- or five-day exploration of the historic shoreline along which New England was founded, driving south from Boston through Plymouth to Cape Cod. Visit Martha's Vineyard and Nantucket before returning through the old whaling capital of New Bedford.

Take Route 3 south, detouring onto Route 3A between Quincy and Kingston. On Cape Cod, follow Routes 6A and 6 to Provincetown, returning via Routes 6 and 28. Return to Boston via I-195, Routes, 140 and 24, and I-93.

The historic South Shore area of Massachusetts is the gateway to Cape Cod and the islands. Just beyond the Boston city limits, off I-93 in **Quincy**, the **Adams National Historical Park** (1250 Hancock St; tel: 617-770-1175) encompasses the birthplaces of the original father-and-son presidential team, John and John Quincy Adams. The Adams's homes are filled with family possessions, including J Q Adams's 14,000-volume **Stone Library**.

As an alternative to busy Route 3, follow Route 3A south for 37 miles (60km) from Quincy, threading though villages such as Cohasset, Scituate, and Duxbury, which all feature a wealth of fine colonial architecture. After joining briefly with Route 3, Route 3A enters **Plymouth**, the Pilgrims' first permanent landing place. The Pilgrims' 1620 landing is commemorated by the country's most famous boulder – Water Street's **Plymouth Rock**. Just a short walk from the rock you will find the **Mayflower II** (State Pier; Apr–Nov: daily 9am–5pm; tel: 508-746 1622). This replica of the Pilgrims' vessel sailed here from England in 1957.

Replica of a Pilgrim Village

Plimoth Plantation (Route. 3A; Apr–Nov: daily 9am–5pm tel: 508-746 1622) is probably the nation's most meticulously researched historical re-creation. This replicated Pilgrim village, *circa* 1627, has thatched roofs, an open-fire cooking facility, and barnyard animals. The costumes of the 'residents,' and their olde English accents are virtually flawless.

To reach Sandwich, the Cape's oldest town, take Route 3 south from Plymouth. After 15 miles (24km), the highway crosses the Cape

Left: a 'resident' of Plimoth Plantation

Cod Canal via the Sagamore Bridge. Follow Route 6A for 3 miles (5km) to the polished little village of **Sandwich**. This might not seem like a center of industry, but the **Sandwich Glass Museum** (129 Main Street; Feb–Dec 9.30am–4.30pm; tel: 508-888 0251) presents room after room of testimony to its 19th-century prowess as a producer of colored glassware. A broader collection of Americana is on display at the nearby **Heritage Plantation** (Grove and Pine streets; mid-May–late Oct daily 10am–5pm; tel: 508-888 3300), a beautifully landscaped complex whose galleries display folk art, militaria, antique automobiles, paintings, and a working carousel from 1912. Back in the village, the **Dan'l Webster Inn** (149 Main Street; tel: 508-888 3622) offers comfortable lodgings.

Nature Trails

The old King's Highway (Route 6A) winds it way east through Cape Cod's prettiest villages. The flavor of this unspoiled corner of the Cape is typified in **Yarmouth Port**, 15 miles (24km) east of Sandwich, where the handsome 1840 Greek Revival **Captain Bangs Hallett House** (11 Strawberry Lane; June–Sept, Sun pm, July–Aug, Thurs pm; tel: 508-362 3021) is filled with the captain's orientalia; out back, nature trails crisscross 50 acres (20ha) of meadow and woods. At **Brewster**, 12 miles (19km) east, there are more trails to explore at the **Cape Cod Museum of Natural History** (Route 6A; Mon–Sat 9.30am–4.30pm, Sun 11am–4.30pm; tel: 508-896 3867). Also in Brewster is **Chillingworth** (Route 6A; tel: 508-896 3640), the Cape's most elegant restaurant. For less formal dining, the stretch of Route 6 that lies ahead offers plenty of roadside seafood restaurants.

The confusingly named 'Lower Cape,' the outer part, begins at **Orleans**, 5 miles (8km) past Brewster. Not far from the town's busy traffic circle are two fine beaches – **Nauset** (Beach Road) on the colder, rougher ocean side; and **Skaket** (Skaket Beach Road), which has a calm bay frontage. Follow Route 6 for 3 miles (5km) north to **Eastham**, where Cape Cod National

Above: skating on a frozen lake in Sandwich

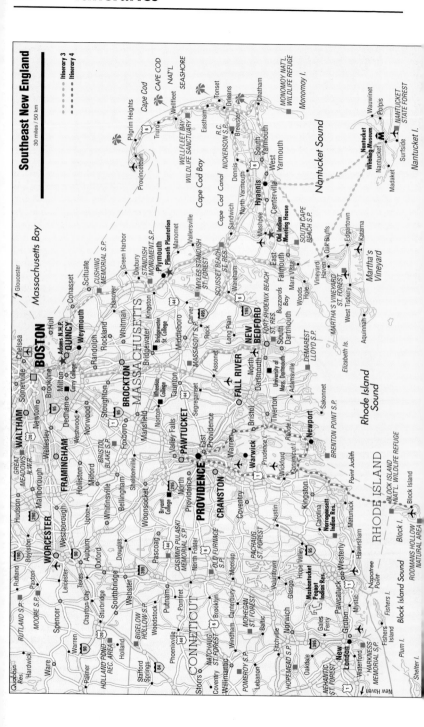

Above Right: Highland Light in Truro
Right: heading for the shore at Cape Cod

Seashore's **Salt Pond Visitors Center** (Doane Road; mid-Feb–Dec daily, Jan–mid Feb weekends only; tel: 508-255 3421) features exhibits and films about the dune lands stretching north for 30 miles (48km) along the Great Beach to Provincetown.

The Pilgrim Monument

From Eastham, by way of the quiet summer resort towns of Wellfleet and Truro, and past the lovely beaches on both bay and ocean sides, it's a 19-mile (31km) drive on Route 6 to **Provincetown**. The Pilgrims briefly anchored here before heading off to Plymouth, an event commemorated by the 252-ft (77-meter) **Pilgrim Monument** (High Pole Hill; daily 9am–4.15pm, July–Aug until 6.15pm; tel: 508-487 1310). It's worth climbing the Monument for views that extend as far as Boston. But the narrow lanes and spirited downtown area below are the main event. The old fishing village has long been an artists' mecca, vacation resort, and focus for a lively gay scene. Commercial Street is lined with boutiques, antiques dealers, galleries, and bistros; the **Provincetown Art Association and Museum** (No 460; tel: 508-487 1750), exhibits the works of generations of painters who were attracted to the area by the Cape's marvelous light.

On the outskirts of town, the **Province Lands Visitors Center** (Race Point Road; Apr–Nov daily 9am–5pm, tel: 508-487 1256) is set in a splendid terrain of undulating dunes, scrub forest laced with bicycle paths, and expansive beaches. At the day's end, settle in at one of the attractive in-town accommodations, such as the **Masthead** (122 Bradford St; tel: 508-675 0880).

The following morning, suitably refreshed, head back to the 'Upper Cape' via Route 6; at Orleans, continue south for 7 miles (11km) on Route 28 to **Chatham**. Quite the antithesis of busy Provincetown, Chatham is a trim, laidback village. Stroll along Main Street, or take a boat ride to the vast, gorgeously desolate **Monomoy National Wildlife Refuge** (Visitors Center,

Morris Island Road; daily 8am–5pm; tel: 508-945 0594).

The highway (Route 28) back to the mainland passes through the busiest and most developed part of the Cape. The main stop along the stretch is **Hyannis** (19 miles/31km west of Chatham), which is famous as the summer residence of the Kennedy family. Here you can catch a ferry connection to Martha's Vineyard (Hy-Line; no cars; May–Oct: tel: 508-778 2600) and Nantucket (Hy-Line; no cars; May–Oct: tel: 508-778 2602; or Steamship Authority; cars and pedestrians; year-round; tel: 508-477 8600).

Another year-round car ferry to Martha's Vineyard is operated by the Steamship Authority (tel: 508-477 8600) out of Woods Hole, 24 miles (39km) west via Route 28. Reservations are recommended both for car ferries and pierside parking.

Martha's Vineyard and Nantucket

Martha's Vineyard looks like a slice of upcountry New England's hills and meadows transported out to sea. The Vineyard has three major centers: Edgartown, Oak Bluffs, and Vineyard Haven. Edgartown presents the most handsome facade, with a number of sea captains' homes, several of which have been converted into upscale inns. Oak Bluffs is more of a family resort. Children love the Flying Horses Carousel, and the toy-like village of Victorian cottages that surrounds the Methodist summer-camp-meeting tabernacle is a cheerful sight. Vineyard Haven is the main commercial center of the island. Beyond the towns, the Vineyard's country lanes are perfect for cyclists. And the sunsets at Aquinnah (formerly known as Gay Head) are legendary.

Nantucket, 30 miles (48km) out to sea, was a whalers' haven in the 19th-century era of *Moby Dick*. Its only real town, Nantucket, reflects those days in its cobblestoned streets, imposing brick mansions, and in the **Whaling Museum** (13 Broad Street; May–Dec; tel: 508-228 1894). The terrain is mostly windswept moorland, surrounded by breathtaking expanses of ocean beach. Like Martha's Vineyard, Nantucket has become an upscale resort island. And, also like the Vineyard, it is wonderful cycling country.

For a brilliant view of New England's maritime history cut north 3 miles (5km) from Hyannis via Route 132 for Route 6. Cross the Sagamore Bridge and, still on Route 6, pick up Route 25 to I-495 for the 27-mile (43km) drive to **New Bedford**. Once the nation's most famous whaling port, New Bedford is known for the 13-block **New Bedford Whaling National Historical Park** (Visitors Center, 33 William Street; daily 9am–4pm; tel: 508-996 4095). Within this old warren of streets stands the **New Bedford Whaling Museum** (18 Johnny Cake Hill; late May–early Sept; tel: 508-997 0046), with exhibits that cover every aspect of the highly dangerous hunt for whales in wooden ships. Check out the half-scale model of one such whaler, and also the skeleton of a blue whale. Opposite the museum, the **Seaman's Bethel** (tel: 508-992 3295) is the sailors' chapel that featured in *Moby Dick* .

Before leaving New Bedford, you might want to savor the area's Portuguese flavor at one of several downtown restaurants that serve authentic cuisine. A good choice is **Antonio's** (267 Coggeshall Street; tel 508-990 3636).

4. NARRAGANSETT BAY *(see maps, p36, 40 & 42)*

A two- or three-day driving tour around scenic Narragansett Bay, taking in Rhode Island's capital, Providence, and the fabulous resort of Newport. An optional ferry excursion leads to unspoiled Block Island.

Starting at Providence, the drive follows Route 114 along the east shore of the bay; at Newport; take Route 138 to cross two bridges and arrive at the west shore. Route 1A heads southward to Point Judith. Return to Providence via 1A north, connecting with Route 1 at Wickford.

For an account of the history of **Providence**, go to the **Roger Williams National Memorial** (282 N. Main Street; daily 9am–4.30pm) in the center of the city. Within walking distance you will find the ornate **Rhode Island State House** (82 Smith St; Mon–Fri 8.30am–4.30pm), topped by the fourth-largest unsupported marble dome in the world. Treasures here include the colony's original charter, and a Gilbert Stuart portrait of George Washington.

On the other side of the Williams Memorial are the campuses of **Brown University** (guided tours daily from admissions office at 45 Prospect Street) and the **Rhode Island School of Design** (RISD). The **Museum of Art** (224 Benefit St; Tues–Sun 10am–5pm, Fri until 8pm) at RISD is strong in French Impressionists, Japanese prints, and 18th-century American decorative arts.

Stroll along **Benefit Street**, which is one of the nation's best-preserved neighborhoods of 18th- and early 19th-century homes. At No 251 is the 1838 Greek Revival **Providence Athenaeum** (tel: 401-421 6970), a library once used by Edgar Allan Poe. The library has a first edition of Audubon's

Above Left: piracy at the Hyannis marina. **Left:** Brant Point Light, Nantucket
Above: Rhode Island State House in Providence

Birds of America. A few blocks to the south, the **John Brown House** (52 Power Street; Mar–Dec Tues–Sat, Sun pm, Jan–Feb weekends only; tel: 401-273 7507) is a superb example of high Georgian architecture. Built for a merchant in 1786, it is filled with period furnishings and China Trade porcelain.

Before leaving Providence, you might opt for a hearty Italian meal at the **Blue Grotto** (210 Atwells Avenue; tel: 401-272 9030) or at one of the other restaurants in 'Little Italy' in Federal Hill. On the city's outskirts, the **Roger Williams Park and Zoo** (Elmwood Ave; daily 9am–5pm, until 4pm in winter) features 150 animals, a planetarium, and rental boats.

Birthplace of the Industrial Revolution

Next on the route is the birthplace of the American Industrial Revolution, in the old factory city of **Pawtucket**, 5 miles (8km) north of Providence

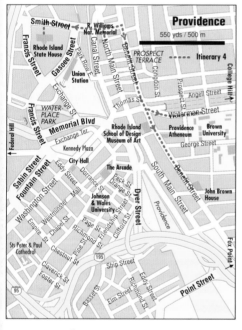

via Route 1 or I-95. **Slater Mill Historic Site** (67 Roosevelt Avenue; tours only; tel: 401-725 8638) preserves the buildings where Samuel Slater introduced America's first water-powered textile machinery in 1793. Among the working displays are antique looms and a waterwheel.

Return to Providence, head east on Route I-195, and pick up Route 114 for the chain of peninsulas and islands that make up the east shore of Narragansett Bay. At **Bristol**, 12 miles (19km) south of I-195, the region's nautical pedigree is celebrated at the **Herreshoff Marine & America's Cup Museum** (1 Burnside Street; tel: 401-253 5000), where a collection of 50 sailing and power boats covers a century of inspired design. Not far away, **Blithewold Mansion and Gardens** (Route. 114; tel: 401-253 2707) is a 45-room summer retreat, built in 1908, surrounded by 33 acres (13ha) of manicured grounds. The spring-bulb display of 50,000 blooms is breathtaking.

Also for horticulturalists is Portsmouth's **Green Animals Topiary Gardens** (Cory's Lane; May–Oct daily 10am–5pm), some 6 miles (10km) south of Bristol. These gardens, which owe much to the mild bay climate and its designers' whimsy, feature any number of creations sculpted from living boxwood, privet, and yew. There's also a small Victorian toy museum on site.

Newport, 8 miles (13km) further south, is the crown jewel of Rhode Island's coast. This is quite an accolade given that Rhode Island, despite being the nation's smallest state, features 400 miles (640km) of coastline. Having grown rich on 18th-century trade, the city blossomed again when Gilded

itineraries

Age magnificoes arrived to outdo each other in building summer 'cottages.' Mostly arrayed along Bellevue Avenue, and all maintained by the Preservation Society of Newport County (tel: 401-847 1000), the greatest of these monuments to pre-income-tax wealth are now open to the public. They include: William Vanderbilt's **Marble House**, which is so ornate that its gold ballroom seems modest; **The Breakers**, Cornelius Vanderbilt II's 70-room Italianate *palazzo*; **Rosecliff**, modeled on Versailles' Grand Trianon; **The Elms**, also French neoclassical in inspiration; **Chateau-sur-Mer**, Victorian Gothic with Renaissance revival interior touches; and Gothic Revival **Belcourt Castle**, the leading light among the cottages in terms of its (European and Asian) art. For an interesting outdoor perspective on the cottages – and striking vistas of Newport's rocky shores – follow **Cliff Walk**, skirting the ocean's edge behind Bellevue Avenue.

America's Oldest Synagogue

There's more to Newport than Gilded Age ostentation. In the heart of the old colonial downtown, the Georgian **Touro Synagogue** (85 Touro Street; tel: 401-847 4794), built in 1763, is the oldest Jewish house of worship in the country. Just outside town, the **Naval War College Museum** (686 Cushing Rd; Mon–Fri 10am–4pm, summer weekends noon–4pm; tel: 401-841 4052) chronicles the history of naval warfare.

Spend the night in Newport's mansion district at the **Ivy Lodge** (12 Clay Street; tel: 401-849 6865) or downtown in the historic **Hotel Viking** (1 Bellevue Avenue; tel: 401-847 3300). For a seafood dinner, try the **Black**

Above: Castle Hill Light, Newport
Right: Beechwood Mansion, Newport

Pearl (Bannister's Wharf; tel: 401-846 5264), popular among the yachting set or, less expensively, the **Mooring** (Sayer's Wharf; tel: 401-846 2260).

Verdant Hills, Tranquil Meadows

After breakfast it's time to head to beautiful **Block Island**. Head for the western shores of Narragansett Bay via Route 138 and the dramatic Newport and Jamestown bridges. On the other side, head south 12 miles (19km) to the fishing port of Point Judith, near the point of departure at **Galilee** for the Block Island ferry (tel: 401-783 4613). Located 12 miles (19km) offshore, where Long Island Sound meets the ocean, Block Island has verdant hills, tranquil marshes, and bluffs rising 200ft (60 meters) above the sea. It also has great beaches and Victorian hotels such as **Atlantic Inn** (High Street; tel: 401-466-5883).

  Scarborough State Beach is one of Rhode Island's best. It is just off Route 1A, which you follow north for 16 miles (26km) to the archetypal New England village of **Wickford**. North of town, off Route 1, **Smith's Castle** (55 Richard Smith Drive; tel: 401-294 3521) is a 1678 plantation house. In the grounds are the graves of colonists killed in King Philip's War.

  Return to Providence (20 miles/ 32km) via Route 1, or I-95. Follow either route south for the Connecticut shore.

Above: Block Island bluffs

5. CONNECTICUT COAST *(see map, p44)*

A two- or three-day ramble along Long Island Sound, with visits to the restored whaling port of Mystic and a Rhode Island seaside resort.

Drive to the New Haven starting point via Route 1 and some side roads; along the Connecticut Valley, the main highways are routes 9, 154, 82, and 156.

At first glance, Connecticut's Long Island Sound shoreline might seem like a crowded corridor for I-95 as it courses between New York City and points east. Soon after turning off the interstate, however, you are bound to find the multifaceted attractions of this short stretch of seacoast.

Yale University is one of **New Haven**'s main claims to fame. Campus attractions include the University Art Gallery, which has a rich collection of early American decorative and contemporary fine art; the Yale Center for British Art; the Beinecke Rare Book and Manuscript Library; and the Peabody Museum of Natural History. For information on any of these contact the Visitors Center (149 Elm Street; tel: 203-432-2300). The campus itself is a classic example of the Ivy League Gothic Revival style of the early 20th century.

Fortify yourself for the day's itinerary at **Louis' Lunch** (263 Crown Street), which is hallowed as the birthplace of the hamburger. Burgers are still a staple at this favorite hangout of generations of Yalies.

Stony Creek, 10 miles (16km) east via routes 1 and 146, is only a tiny seaside village but it is the embarkation point for a boat trip to the Thimble Islands. Board the *Sea Mist II* (Thimble Island Rd; tel: 203-488 8905) for a fascinating narrated tour of the islands – a scattering of 354 rugged outcrops peppered with unlikely mansions, summer homes on stilts, and stories dating back to Captain Kidd. **Hammonasset State Beach**, 15 miles (24km) farther along routes 146 and 1, is Connecticut's largest waterfront state park. It occupies an entire peninsula, with ample room for swimming, surfcasting (fishing from the shore), hiking, and camping.

The Nation's Oldest Inn

The town of **Essex**, 15 miles (24km) farther east (via Route 1 and, for a short stretch, north along Route 9) typifies upscale Yankeedom. Check out the restored 18th-century homes, a riverfront dotted with sailboats, and the rambling **Griswold Inn** (36 Main Street; tel: 860-767 1776), built in 1776 and alleged to be the oldest continuously operating inn in the US. Stroll down to the wharfside **Connecticut River Museum** (67 Main Street; Tues–Sun 10am–5pm), which has a working model of a Revolutionary War submarine.

To reach the town of East Haddam, you can travel on the **Essex Steam Train** (1 Railroad Avenue; tel: 860-767 0103 or 1-800-ESSEX TRAIN) which,

Right: the Ivy League Yale University is one of New Haven's main claims to fame

drawn by a 1926 locomotive, clatters north along the Connecticut to Deep River Landing. From here you can continue by boat to East Haddam's riverside Victorian **Goodspeed Opera House** (Route 82; tel: 860-873 8664).

If you would rather drive, take Route 154 north from Essex to Route 82 east – a journey of eight miles (13km). Aside from the Opera House, East Haddam's main attraction is **Gillette Castle State Park** (67 River Road; open Memorial Day–Labor Day Fri–Sun 10am–5pm). You can visit the imposing stone 'castle,' which was constructed in 1914 by actor William Gillette.

American Impressionists

For a more evocative view of the region's golden past, drive south from East Haddam on routes 82 and 156, which pass through the peaceful countryside that borders Connecticut's west shore. The **Florence Griswold Museum** (96 Lyme Street; Apr–Dec Tues–Sat 10am–5pm, Sun 1–5pm, Jan–Mar Wed–Sun 1–5pm; tel: 860-434 5542) in **Old Lyme** (15 miles/24km south) recalls Old Lyme's heyday as an artists' colony at the start of the 20th century, and has a collection of American Impressionist paintings.

In **New London**, 15 miles (24km) east of Old Lyme at the mouth of the Thames River (Route 154 meanders along the coast; Route 1 is faster), is the US Coast Guard's training academy, where the magnificent sailing

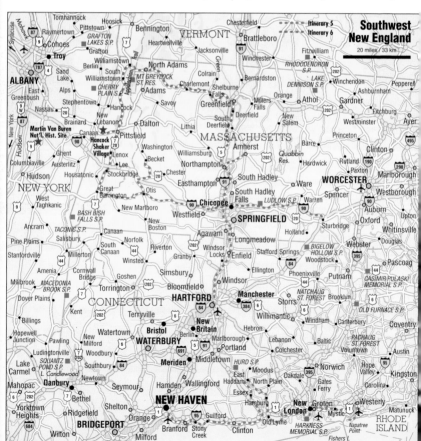

vessel *Eagle* is used for training coast guard cadets (tours Fri–Sun when the *Eagle* is in port; tel: 860-444 8270). The nearby **Coast Guard Museum** (Mohegan Avenue; daily 10am–5pm), tells of 200 years of coastal defense and lifesaving.

In **Groton**, on the other side of the Thames, the **USS *Nautilus* Memorial** (1 Crystal Lake Road; Wed–Mon, Tues pm; tel: 860-694 3174) offers tours of the USA's first nuclear submarine.

Living History at Mystic

Mystic, 6 miles (10km) east of Groton, is a highlight of the state's coast. **Mystic Seaport** (75 Greenmanville Avenue; daily 9am–5pm; winter 10am–4pm) at the mouth of the Mystic River is a 17-acre (7ha) living history museum where you will find early 19th-century wharves, stores and houses. Costumed interpreters demonstrate crafts and cooking techniques. The collection of some 500 vessels includes the *Charles W. Morgan* (the last surviving wooden whaling ship), and a replica of the infamous *Amistad* slave ship.

Mystic's other major attraction is the **Mystic Aquarium** (55 Coogan Boulevard; July–Labor Day daily 9am–6pm,off season 9am–5pm), which has more than 6,000 marine specimens, including any number of seals, sea lions, and beluga whales. The aquarium is now also the home of the high-tech **Institute for Exploration**, with exhibits and a simulated deep-sea dive devised by Robert Ballard, who played a key role in raising the *Titanic*.

Mystic offers dozens of dining and lodging choices. **Whaler's Inn** (20 E. Main Street; tel: 860-536 1506) has an Italian restaurant; **Mystic Pizza** (56 W. Main Street) was the model for the 1988 movie of that name, starring Julia Roberts. Alternatively, head 15 miles (24km) east across the Rhode Island border to **Watch Hill**, a quaint resort dominated by immense summer homes built 100 years ago. To work up an appetite for dinner, you might check out the **Flying Horse Carousel** (Bay Street; summer daily 1–8pm), a Watch Hill attraction since the 1860s, or embark on the mile-long (1.6km) walk along the **Napatree Point** sandy spit. If you have a weakness for seafood and luscious desserts, head for the 1916 period-piece **Olympia Tea Room** (30 Bay Street; Apr–Oct). From the Mystic–Watch Hill area, it's easy to hop onto I-95 for New Haven or Providence.

Above: Old Lyme still attracts artists
Right: excavations on the beach

6. BERKSHIRE HILLS *(see map, p44)*

A two- to five-day driving tour through Massachusetts' gently rolling Berkshire Hills and Pioneer Valley, with stops at the Old Sturbridge Village living history museum, and in Connecticut's capital, Hartford.

From Springfield, follow routes 20 and 23 to Great Barrington; then head in a northward direction along Route 7 and side roads. Return via Route 2 eastward and Route 5 southward, along the Connecticut River valley.

The Berkshire Hills are far less rugged than the mountains of Vermont and New Hampshire, but they do incorporate a refreshing variety of scenery. Benefiting from their proximity to the cosmopolitan centers of Boston and New York, the hills have, in recent decades, become famous as a summer arts venue. The Pioneer Valley, named for the 17th-century settlers of the area, forms the eastern gateway to the region and its largest city, **Springfield**.

Due to its location on the conveniently navigable Connecticut River, Springfield was selected as the site of the first US arsenal. The **Springfield Armory National Historic Site** (Tues–Sun 10am–4.30pm; tel: 413-734 85510 tells the story of nearly 200 years of armament manufacturing. Springfield is also famous as the birthplace of basketball. The **Naismith Memorial Basketball Hall of Fame** (1150 West Columbus Avenue; 10am–5pm; tel: 413-781 6500), named for Dr James Naismith, who invented the sport in 1891, honors great players and offers interactive exhibits.

In downtown Springfield, four good museums cater to different tastes (State and Chestnut streets; all Wed–Sun noon–4pm). The **Connecticut Valley Historical Museum** focuses on local history, the **George Walter Vincent Smith Art Museum** is strong in Japanese art, armor, and decorative items; the **Museum of Fine Arts** exhibits American and French Impressionist works, and the **Springfield Science Museum** has interactive displays for children.

Festive Dance

If it's summer and you are a dance aficionado, it is well worth catching the **Jacob's Pillow Dance Festival**. (George Cantor Road at Route 20; tel:

413-637 1322 or 413-243 0745). Drive west from Springfield on Route 20 for 16 miles (26km) to join Route 23, leading westward into the hilly, forested heart of the Berkshires. At Otis, 15 miles (24km) west on Route 23, turn north after eight miles (13km) on Route 8 to reach Becket, where the festival takes place between May and August. For 10 weeks every year, ballet, modern, and folk troupes perform on indoor and outdoor stages.

For an upscale resort, try **Great Barrington** (15 miles/24km west of Otis, Route 23 then Route 7, the Berkshires' main north–south highway). The town has a large number of antique shops and intimate restaurants such as the **Helsinki Tea Company** (284 Main Street; tel: 413-528 3394). Great Barrington is set in natural splendor: **Bartholomew's Cobble**

Left: maintaining the tradition of the early Patriots

(Route 7A) is a rocky riverside glade with hiking trails and a natural history museum (tel: 413-229 8600); **Mt Washington State Forest** (Route 23), with its 50ft (15-meter) **Bash Bish Falls** draws hikers and campers.

Norman Rockwell's Small-town America

Head north on Route 7 for 7 miles (11km) to **Stockbridge**, where the artist Norman Rockwell, chronicler of small-town America, lived for 25 years prior to his death in 1978. Main Street looks much as it did when Rockwell painted it. To see the world's largest collection of original Rockwells, travel two miles out of town to the **Norman Rockwell Museum** (Route 183; daily 10am–5pm; tel: 413-298 4100). The sculptor Daniel Chester French, who created the Lincoln Memorial in Washington DC, had a home and studio at **Chesterwood** (Williamsville Road; May–Oct daily 10am–5pm; tel: 413-298 3579), where you can see his casts and models. The diplomat Joseph Choate also lived here. His mansion **Naumkeag** (S. Prospect Hill; Memorial Day–Columbus Day daily 10am–4.15pm; tel: 413-298 3239), dating to 1886 and designed by Stanford White, has a fine collection of Chinese porcelain, and spectacular gardens. Just out of town, the **Historic Merrell Inn** (Route 102, S. Lee; tel: 413-243 1794) is a good place to put up for the night.

To experience the essence of the Berkshires, head for **Lenox**, 8 miles (13km) north of Stockbridge on Route 7A (off Route 7). Every year Lenox hosts the **Tanglewood Music Festival** *(see Calendar of Events, page 79)*, at which international luminaries perform with the Boston Symphony. An evening spent listening to a concert on the lawn at Tanglewood can be an unforgettable experience.

Novelist Edith Wharton built her Georgian Revival summer home in Lenox in 1902. **The Mount** (Plunkett Street; late May–Oct daily 9am–3pm; tel: 413-637 1899) bears testimony to the writer's uncluttered interior design. Another writer spent some of his most productive years in **Pittsfield**, 6 miles

Above: in the grounds of Naumkeag
Right: the past is omnipresent in New England

(10km) north of Lenox on Route 7. Herman Melville completed *Moby Dick* in 1850 at his farmhouse **Arrowhead** (780 Holmes Road; Memorial Day–Oct daily 10am–5pm; tel: 413-442 1793). Books, papers and Melville memorabilia are displayed at the **Berkshire Athenaeum** (1 Wendell Avenue; open daily; tel: 413-443 7171).

Home of the Shakers

More 19th-century artifacts can be found 6 miles (10km) west of Pittsfield, via Route 20, at **Hancock Shaker Village** (Route 20; winter 10am–3pm, summer 9.30am–5pm; tel: 413-443 0188). This site constitutes one of the best-preserved reminders of the Shaker religious movement which, having originated in England in 1747, peaked in the

US in the early 19th century. The buildings, farm, and a store selling Shaker reproduction furniture illustrate the sect's devotion to orderly simplicity, in a bucolic setting typical of that chosen by Shaker communities in New England.

The drive to **Williamstown** passes the state's highest point. Continuing on Route 7 for 22 miles (35km) north from Pittsfield, watch for the right-hand turnoff to the **Mt Greylock Reservation**; the 3,500ft (1,065-meter) summit is accessible by trail or auto road. In Williamstown, a trim village that has been home to Williams College since 1793, the **Sterling and Francine Clark Art Institute** (225 South Street; tel: 413-458 9545) has a splendid collection of French Impressionists crowned by more than 30 Renoirs.

Art in an unlikely setting is the main attraction 10 miles (16km) east via Route 2 in **North Adams**, an old industrial town long overshadowed by Williamstown's Ivy League image. Now that a former factory compound has

been converted into the **Massachusetts Museum of Contemporary Arts** (87 Marshall Street; daily 10am–6pm; tel: 413-664 4481), North Adams attracts enthusiasts of modern painting, sculpture, and performance art.

The scenic, 30-mile (48km) drive east to Greenfield on Route 2 begins with an improbably sharp 'fiddler's elbow' turn just outside North Adams. Along the way, the delightful little village of **Shelburne Falls** (just off Route 2, 22 miles/35km east of North Adams) features one of the region's most unusual attractions – the **Bridge of Flowers**, an old trolley bridge that is now a pedestrian walkway festooned with blossoms. At Greenfield, head south 3 miles (5km) on Route 5 to reach Deerfield. The beautifully preserved **Historic Deerfield** (The Street; daily 9.30am–4.30pm; tel: 413-774 5581) commemorates the life of New England pioneers, in particular the horrific Deerfield Raid, a bloody attack by French troops and their Indian allies in 1704. Deerfield's historical legacy can be seen in individual period homes, and at the **Flynt Center of Early New England Life** and **Memorial Hall Museum**. The Deerfield Inn, dating to 1884, provides excellent food and lodging.

A 30-mile (48km) drive south to **Springfield** along Route 5 or I-91 leads through Pioneer Valley and a landscape thick with college towns and their attendant bookstores, cafes, and cultural offerings. **Northampton** is the home of Smith College, a liberal arts institution for women. Eight miles (13km) east on Route 9 is **Amherst**, where both Amherst College and the much larger University of Massachusetts lend a youthful atmosphere to the environment. Amherst's **Emily Dickinson Homestead** (280 Main Street; guided tours only; tel: 413-542 8161) preserves the belongings of the poet who lived in the town throughout her life (1830–86).

Old Sturbridge Village, 31 miles (50km) to the east of Springfield via I-90 (1 Old Sturbridge Village Road; tel: 508-347 3362) constitutes New England's premier period restoration. Comprising more than 40 structures transported here from sites throughout the region, it reproduces small town life *circa* 1830. Craftspeople – including weavers, cobblers, blacksmiths, and printers – in recreated surroundings appear in period clothing and a local store stocks merchandise representing the range of goods on sale in that era.

State Capital

Connecticut's capital, **Hartford**, 26 miles (42km) south of Springfield via I-91, has two attractions that are both well worth seeing. **Mark Twain House** (351 Farmington Avenue; tel: 860-493 6411), dating to 1874, is a magnificent, quirky mansion decorated by Louis Tiffany and replete with the great writer's furnishings and memorabilia. The **Wadsworth Athenaeum** (600 Main Street; tel: 860-247 0998) is a gallery featuring baroque, Impressionist, and 19th-century American works, and an impressive collection of 17th-century American furniture. If you have time you might also want to visit the **State Capitol** (210 Capitol Avenue; Mon–Fri 9am–3pm; tel: 860-240 0222). The building overlooks the lovely, Olmstead-designed **Bushnell Park**, where a carousel from 1914 is open for rides from April through September.

Above Left: Northampton's Smith College of Liberal Arts is exclusive to women.
Left: the archetypal image of New England in fall. **Above:** Bridge of Flowers detail

7. GREEN MOUNTAINS, VERMONT *(see map, p52)*

A two-day driving tour through the bucolic heart of leafy Vermont, staying overnight in Stowe Mountain Resort.

Follow Route 30 from Brattleboro to Route 100, Vermont's scenic north-south 'Main Street.' Most of the itinerary follows 100, except for a central portion. Head north and west over the final miles via routes 108 and 15.

Nearly every image conjured by the name 'Vermont' comes to life along this route between the southeastern and northwestern corners of the state –

trim little villages, rolling dairy farms dotted with black-and-white cows, and the rugged slopes of the Green Mountains. The spectacular fall colors are world-famous.

Begin this itinerary at **Brattleboro**, on the banks of the Connecticut River, near the site of Vermont's first permanent settlement, founded in 1724. In the 19th century the town became a busy manufacturing center. The lively downtown mixes workaday businesses with the bookstores and bistros established by newcomers in the 1960s. Aspects of counterculture life can still be found at Common Ground (25 Elliott Street), an upstairs earthy health-food hangout. The **Brattleboro Museum and Art Center** (Vernon and Main streets; Tues–Sun noon–6pm) recounts local history, and hosts changing art exhibitions.

For the 50-mile (80km) drive to Weston, follow Route 30 along the West River valley, heading north at Rawsonville onto Route 100. En route the towns of Newfane, Townshend, and Jamaica are fine examples of compact Vermont settlements centered on village greens. **Newfane**, which is particularly proud of its 1825 Greek Revival county courthouse, is big on antique shops, and on summer Sundays there is a flea market.

The Longest Bridge

The **Scott Covered Bridge**, about 2 miles (3km) north of Townshend, spans the West River. Built in 1870 and now open only to pedestrians, the 275ft (85 meter) structure is the longest covered bridge without a center support in the state. Bridges were traditionally covered to protect their frames from the elements and not, as some people say, to pacify skittish horses.

Routes 30 and 100 converge at East Jamaica, and continue together for 8 miles (13km) along the eastern boundary of the Green Mountain National Forest. At Rawsonville, continue north along Route 100 through the heart of southern Vermont's ski country, with the slopes of Stratton Mountain looming above. For panoramic vistas, go west on Route 30 at Rawsonville to ride **Stratton's aerial gondola** (Route 1; tel: 802-297 2200) to the peak.

Weston, one of the first isolated Vermont towns to be revived as a bucolic

Above: on the streets of Woodstock. **Above Right:** the place for bric-a-brac and curios
Right: Newfane is proud of the historic, 19th-century buildings facing the town green

ideal, lies 12 miles (19km) ahead on Route 100. The route dips down along the banks of West River before climbing into the hills at Londonderry. Weston's ample town green is circled by homes dating back to the 1790s. On the green, the **Weston Playhouse** (tel: 802-824 5288) has hosted summer theater for more than 60 years. But most visitors are drawn to Weston by the **Vermont Country Store**, a throwback to the small-town emporia of a century ago. With a potbellied stove and a penny-candy counter, the store has grown into an *omnium-gatherum* of all sorts of practical items.

When it comes to lunch, the Bryant House restaurant next to the store is a good bet, especially if you have a big appetite. If you are staying the night, the Inn at Weston (Route 100; tel: 802-824 6789) has comfortable rooms and fine dining.

The Boyhood Haunts of Calvin Coolidge

Calvin Coolidge was one of two US presidents born in Vermont (the other was Chester A Arthur). Coolidge's ancestral village of Plymouth Notch, located in the hills 32 miles (51km) north of Weston via routes 100 and 100A, is preserved as the **Plymouth Notch Historic District** (mid-May–mid-Oct daily 9.30am–5pm). Here you can see his boyhood haunts, such as his father's general store, and the family's cheese company. Particularly inter-sting is the house in which he took the oath of office on August 2, 1923, when, as vice-president, he learned of President Harding's death. A dyed-in-the-wool conservative Yankee, Coolidge would doubtless approve if he could see how little Plymouth Notch has changed.

It's another Vermont altogether at **Woodstock**, 17 miles (27km) east of Plymouth Notch via routes 100A and 4. The roaring Ottauquechee River once powered woolen mills. It was on a hillside near here in 1934 that the state's first ski tow presaged Vermont's modern tourist economy. Also instrumental in Woodstock's transformation was Laurence Rockefeller's acquisition of the Woodstock Inn (Route 4, tel: 1-800 894 6327 or 802-234 9999), which he turned into one of Vermont's plushest hostelries.

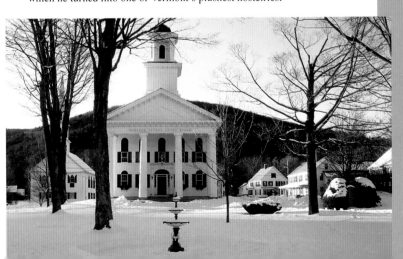

Another of his local legacies is **Marsh-Billings-Rockefeller National Park** (Route 12; June–Oct daily). This 500-acre (200-ha) woodland tract honors George Perkins Marsh, a 19th-century Woodstock native and early conservationist who advised the property's owner, the railroad magnate and gentleman farmer Frederick Billings. Nearby is the **Billings Farm and Museum** (Route 12; May–late Oct daily 10am–5pm), a working model farm since Billings's day. In addition to its prize dairy herd the attraction features an excellent collection of antique farm implements and exhibits chronicling the history of local agriculture.

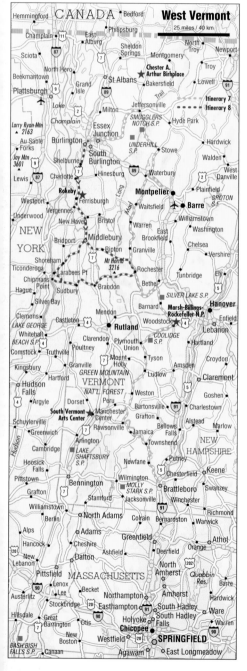

Woodstock's town center, a sophisticated place of galleries, boutiques, and cafes, is surrounded by block after block of handsomely restored Federal and Greek Revival homes. For lunch you might try Pane e Salute (61 Central Street), which specializes in fresh-baked Italian bread and pizzas.

Melancholy Scenery

Head north out of Woodstock on Route 12, through lush pastures belonging to today's gentleman and lady farmers, and pick up Route 107 for a quick swing west to Route 100. Follow this highway north through a typically scenic Vermont landscape. For 35 miles (56km) between Stockbridge and Waitsfield, 100 again hugs the rugged National Forest; no left turn hereabouts will leave you on level ground for long. The scenery becomes almost melancholy as you pass through Granville Gulf, which is so steep that the sun barely penetrates to the road.

Waitsfield and Warren (just to the south) are service towns for the Sugarbush and Mad River Glen ski areas. To visit Montpelier, the US's smallest state capital, turn east on I-89, 12 miles (19km) north of Waitsfield, and continue for 10 miles (16km). In **Montpelier**, the gold-domed 1836 **Vermont State House** (115 State Street; Mon–Fri 8am–4pm; tel: 802-828 2228) and **Vermont Historical Society** (109 State Street;Tues–Fri 9am–4.30pm, Sat until 4pm, Sun pm only; tel: 802-828 2291) are worth a look. Otherwise, continue north on Route 100. Just past I-89, the **Ben & Jerry's Factory** (tel: 1-802 244 8687) offers tours for lovers of the Vermont-made ice cream.

Vermont's Highest Peak

Stowe village,10 miles (16km) north, back on Route 100, is nestled beneath Mt Mansfield, Vermont's highest peak at 4,400ft (1,340 meters). Stowe was a quiet dairy community until the 1930s when the first trails were cut on Mansfield. In the 1950s and '60s the town boomed and today **Stowe Mountain Resort** is one of the East Coast's finest ski areas. Most retail establishments, restaurants, and accommodations are situated on Route 108, the 'Mountain Road' that leads up to the slopes. The village comprises just a few streets, busy year-round with stores selling everything Vermont, from maple syrup to locally made Tubbs snowshoes, and with snug bistros such as the Blue Moon Cafe (35 School Street). You can stay in town at the Green Mountain Inn (1 Main Street; tel: 802-253 7301), a local landmark since the 1830s; or head north out of town to the Trapp Family Lodge (Luce Hill Road; tel: 802-253 8511 or 1-800 826 7000), founded and still run by the von Trapps of *The Sound of Music* fame. The lodge offers a network of cross-country ski trails.

Continue up the Mountain Road north of Stowe to reach the year-round **aerial gondola** and summer auto toll road (tel: 802-253 3000) up Mt Mansfield, where summit views range across New York State, New Hampshire, and Quebec. Keep heading north, and you will wend your way through Smugglers' Notch (road open late spring through mid-fall; otherwise head to Burlington via Route 100 south and I-89). The narrow, tortuous road crests at 2,160ft (660 meters), amid towering ledges where peregrine falcons nest, and where hiking trails lead to the summit of Mt Mansfield.

The biggest attraction along the 18-mile (29km) drive from Stowe to Route 15 at Jeffersonville is **Smugglers Notch Resort** (tel: 802-644 8851), a three-mountain ski area and year-round family resort. You will find hiking and mountain-biking trails, horseback riding, and a water park. At Jeffersonville, turn west onto Route 15 for the 30-mile (48km) drive to Burlington. A turnoff at Underhill for **Underhill State Park** leads to a web of trails that ascend Mt Mansfield. At Burlington, pick up I-89 to return to southern Vermont; or proceed with the Burlington and Champlain Valley itinerary *(see page 54)*.

Above: snowboarding is one of many winter sports to be found in Vermont

8. Burlington and
Lake Champlain Valley *(see map, p52)*

A two- or three-day itinerary taking in Vermont's largest and most diverse city, and a ramble through the broad Champlain valley. After a stop in the college town of Middlebury, follow side roads to Lake Champlain and through lofty passes in the Green Mountains.

The drive follows Route 7 south from Burlington, then loops toward Lake Champlain and back via routes 30, 74, and 73. Routes 73, 100, and 125 complete the circuit through the mountains and back to Middlebury.

Burlington, known as Vermont's 'Queen City,' enjoys a beautiful hillside location facing the broadest part of Lake Champlain. The city's cultural life is enriched by three major colleges, most notably the University of Vermont (UVM). The hilltop **UVM campus** is a good place from which to begin exploring the city. Along University Place stand an array of college buildings,

including the 1825 Old Mill (whose cornerstone was laid by the Marquis de Lafayette), and architect H H Richardson's Romanesque 1886 Billings Student Center. Around the corner is the **Fleming Museum** (61 Colchester Avenue; Tues–Fri 9am–4pm, Sat and Sun 1–5pm; tel:802-656 0750), with an excellent collection of European and American art, complemented by ethnographic exhibits, including an Egyptian mummy.

Walk down College or Main Street to Burlington's lively downtown. The neighborhood is dominated by the pedestrians-only Church Street Marketplace with its bistros, boutiques, and craft galleries. The most interesting gallery is probably the **Vermont Craft Center at Frog Hollow** at No 86, which exhibits works by Vermont artisans. For lunch or dinner stop in at Leunig's, one of several seasonal Church Street sidewalk cafes, at the corner of College Street.

Burlington's waterfront has been reclaimed after years of neglect; the lakeside path makes for a good stroll or cycle ride. Here are piers from which you can take a ferry (King Street Landing; tel: 802-864 9804) to New York State or a trip on the *Spirit of Ethan Allen II* (Burlington Community Boathouse; tel: 802-862 8300). Also at the waterfront is the **Lake Champlain Basin Science Center** (College Street; mid-June–Labor Day daily 11am–5pm, rest of year: weekends only; tel: 802-864 1848), where exhibits such as aquarium tanks explain the natural history of the 125-mile (200km) long lake.

An Exhibition of Americana
Once you have seen enough of Burlington, head south on Route 7. After 10 miles (16km) you will hit **Shelburne**, where the **Shelburne Museum** (Route 7; late May–late Oct daily 10am–5pm; tel: 802-985 3346) comprises one of the nation's premier collections of Americana. Largely the legacy of heiress Electra Havemeyer Webb, the museum's vast holdings

Above: on Burlington Bay, Lake Champlain

include American fine and folk art, toys and tools, horse-drawn vehicles, and much more, all arrayed among 37 buildings on 45 landscaped acres (18 ha). One of the museum's biggest attractions is the *Ticonderoga*, a nearly 100-year-old Lake Champlain passenger steamer hauled here by rail in the early 1950s and lovingly restored.

Shelburne Farms (Harbor and Bay roads; daily 10am–5pm; tel: 802-985 8686) was the Webbs' country estate. Now a model farm, it conducts tours of its cheesemaking and other enterprises. Children love the animals in the petting zoo. The 1880s Farm and Breeding Barns are magnificent, and the 110-room main house is now the **Inn at Shelburne Farms** (tel: 802-985 8123).

Fugitive Slaves

Panoramic vistas of Lake Champlain and the surrounding farmlands open up to the west along Route 7 south of Shelburne. At **Ferrisburgh**, stop in at **Rokeby** (Route 7; tel: 802-877 3406), home of 19th-century writer Rowland Robinson. This unpretentious farmhouse is believed to have been a stop on the 'underground railroad,' where the staunchly abolitionist author helped escaped slaves make their way to freedom in Canada.

At **Vergennes**, a small town with a delightful Victorian downtown 14 miles (23km) south of Shelburne, turn west via Basin Harbor Road to visit the **Lake Champlain Maritime Museum** (Panton Road; mid-May–late Oct daily 10am–5pm; tel: 802-475 2022). The exhibits, including a collection of antique water craft, relate the history of navigation on the lake. Don't miss the replica of the *Philadelphia*, a Revolutionary War gunboat. Down the road is the **Basin Harbor Club** (Panton Road; tel: 802-475 2311), an exclusive lakeside resort.

Middlebury, 13 miles (21km) south of

Above: dining on Burlington's Church Street
Right: lighthouse at the Shelburne Museum

Vergennes via Route 7, is an archetypal New England college town. On its western edge, the campus of **Middlebury College**, a 200-year-old liberal arts institution, features a **Center for the Arts** (Route 30; Tues–Fri 10am–5pm, weekends noon–5pm; tel: 802-443 6433) with works by Rodin. Middlebury has more than a small town's usual share of shops and eateries: within a few blocks are the Vermont State Craft Center at Frog Hollow (1 Mill St); and Woody's (5 Bakery Lane) – a pleasant riverside restaurant (in season ask for a table on the terrace). Also downtown, in an 1829 quarry magnate's house, is the **Sheldon Museum** (1 Park Street; Mon–Sat 10am–5pm; tel: 802-388 2117) with folk art, furniture, and artifacts from 19th-century Vermont.

Middlebury's most impressive building is the 1809 **Congregational Church**. Its steeple, which might well be the finest in the state, rises 135ft (40 meters) in four tiers, and includes a graceful octagonal belfry. Up the hill, facing the town green, is the brick, 1827 Middlebury Inn (14 Courthouse Square; tel: 802-388 4563), one of Vermont's most gracious inns. It makes for a good stopover, although traffic noise can be a problem if you sleep with the windows open.

Horse Power

To see some handsome examples of the state's official animal, the Morgan horse, take a 4-mile (6-km) detour north, via routes 125 and 23, to the University of Vermont's **Morgan Horse Farm** (74 Battell Drive, Weybridge; May–Oct daily 9am–5pm; tel: 802-388 2011). You can observe the sturdy, beautifully proportioned Morgans in their stalls, watch them graze in rolling pastures, and learn how the breed originated, and how it acquired its status.

Traveling through some of Vermont's lushest dairy lands, head southwest out of Middlebury via routes 30 and 74, for 13 miles (21km), to **Shoreham**.

The town is famous for its apple crop – in early fall several local orchards let you pick your own apples, and sell delicious fresh-pressed cider. Continue another 5 miles (8km) to Larabees Point if you would like to take the short ferry crossing (tel: 802-897 7999) to Ticonderoga, New York, site of historic **Fort Ticonderoga** (May 21–Oct 21 9am–5pm; tel: 518-585 2821). This bastion was captured from the British in 1775 by Vermont icon Ethan Allen.

To see another Revolutionary War site continue along the Vermont side of Lake Champlain. Follow Route 73 for 6 miles (10km) south from Larabees Point to Orwell, turn right and head another 6 miles west to Chipman's Point and **Mt Independence** (grounds: daily; Visitors Center: Memorial Day–Columbus Day Wed–Sun 9.30am–5.30pm; tel: 802-948 2000). This historic attraction concentrates on an American fort that commanded the lake in the battle against the British. Various exhibits at the Visitors Center relate the story, and marked trails point out the remaining earthworks.

If you enjoy driving, Vermont's rugged beauty rewards the time you spend behind the wheel. Retrace your route back to Route 73, cross Route 22A and pass through the one-street town of Orwell. Continue on Route 73 through Sudbury to **Brandon** on busy north–south Route 7. Throughout the 13-mile (21km) drive from Orwell to Brandon, the Green Mountains loom in front of you.

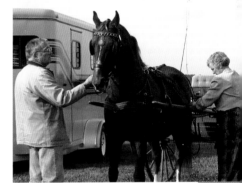

Hiking Up Mt Horrid

If you want to rest for the night in Brandon, a recommended stop is the Lilac Inn (53 Park Street; tel: 802-247 5463), on a street of grand 19th-century homes. Either way, rejoin Route 73, which climbs into the heart of the Green Mountain National Forest. The highest point, at 2,200ft (660 meters), along the winding 17-mile (27km) road to Route 100 is at **Brandon Gap**. The **Long Trail**, Vermont's 'Footpath through the Wilderness,' which crosses the road here, affords hiking access to the 3,220 ft (1,000-meter) summit of Mt Horrid to the north.

From the intersection of Route 73 with Route 100, follow 100 for five miles (8km) north to Hancock, then turn left for the 21-mile (34km) drive toward Middlebury on Route 125. Heading west, follow a steep route through rugged terrain that peaks at the 2,150ft (650-meter) **Middlebury Gap**. Halfway between Hancock and the Gap is a right-hand turnoff for Texas Falls, a beautiful cascade on the Hancock Branch of the White River. Continuing across the Gap, Route 125 descends into **Ripton**, the one-time summer home of Robert Frost. At the **Robert Frost Wayside Area**, a trail leads for a mile (1.6 km) through terrain reminiscent of the poet's work; quotes from his works are spaced along the trail. At Middlebury, connect with Route 7 to return north to Burlington, or head south along this, a primary artery of western Vermont.

Above Left: hiker on the Long Trail, Vermont's 'Footpath through the Wilderness'
Left: picture-postcard Vermont in the fall. **Above:** a 16-year-old Morgan horse

9. LAKE WINNIPESAUKEE REGION, NEW HAMPSHIRE *(see map below)*

A one-day circuit of the lakes, with stops for cruises, crafts, and museums.

The drive follows Route 11 up the west shore of Lake Winnipesaukee, and skirts Squam Lake via routes 3 and 113. Follow Route 109 along Winnipesaukee's east shore and return to your starting place via Route 28.

Begin at **Wolfeboro**, near Lake Winnipesaukee's southeast corner. The lake, dotted with hundreds of islands and surrounded by steep ranges of forested

hills, shimmers at the heart of New Hampshire. It is 28 miles (45km) long, and has a raggedly indented shoreline that stretches for nearly 300 miles (480km). Wolfeboro, the largest lakeside town, calls itself 'America's oldest summer resort.' The New Hampshire governor, John Wentworth, built a summer retreat here in 1769, and artifacts from the long-vanished Wentworth mansion are exhibited at the **Libby Museum** (Route 109; tel: 603-569 1035), overlooking Winter Harbor.

Dentist Henry Libby built the museum in 1912 for his collections of curiosities, including Abenaki Indian maps and drawings, and a 350-year-old canoe. Nearby, the **New Hampshire Antique and**

Above: canoeing, Lake Winnipesaukee

Classic Boat Museum (Route 28; Mon–Sat 10am–4pm, Sun noon–4pm; tel: 603-569 4554) recounts the history of pleasure boating in the region. Also pertaining to recent history is the summer resort of **Alton Bay**. Follow Route 28 south for 10 miles (16km) to the town, which is tucked at the end of a long finger of Lake Winnipesaukee. It offers concerts at the outdoor bandstand and cheap lunches at Shibley's Drive-In Restaurant (Route 11). Head up the west side of Winnipesaukee on Route 11. Break the 11-mile (18km) drive to Weirs Beach at **Mt Major State Forest**, where a 1½-mile trail leads to the 1,800ft (550 meter) summit, and great views.

Weirs Beach is the flashiest of Lake Winnipesaukee resort towns, and a godsend if you're traveling with children – here are video arcades, bowling alleys, and water slides. This is the home port of the MV *Mount Washington* (tel: 603-366 5531 or 1-800 THE MOUNT), an 1888 steamship (now diesel) that has served as a pleasure cruiser here since 1940. The 200ft (60-meter) boat serenely threads its way past the lake's islands. If you want to stick to the shore, there's a nice public beach at **Endicott Park**.

Meredith, 4 miles (6km) north of Weirs Beach via Route 3, offers a shift in character: here the emphasis is on craft boutiques and art galleries. There are waterfront inns, restaurants, and stores in the **Inns and Marketplace at Mills Falls** (Route 3; tel: 603-279 7006), housed in a former textile mill. The Waterfall Cafe at the top of the waterfalls serves a good light lunch.

On Golden Pond was Filmed Here

Continue north on Route 3 to **Squam Lake**, New Hampshire's second-largest body of water. **Holderness** is the main town here and, like Squam Lake itself, its image contrasts sharply with the tourist-oriented west shore of Winnipesaukee. This is the genteel, old-money summer milieu captured in the 1981 film *On Golden Pond*, which was filmed right here.

For the **Science Center of New Hampshire** (May–Oct daily 9.30am–4.30pm; tel: 603-968 7194) – a 200-acre (80 ha) preserve featuring native wildlife in a woodland setting, trails, interactive exhibits, and animal programs – turn right onto Route 113. Board the Center's pontoon boat for a **Loon Cruise**. The black-and-white birds with the unearthly 'laugh' are prized Squam residents, and watching them dive and call is quite a thrill.

For 13 miles (21km) after Holderness, Route 113 winds through pretty countryside. At the intersection of 113 and Route 109 is the trim little village of **Center Sandwich**. This is where the League of New Hampshire Craftsmen (represented in stores throughout the state) was launched more than 70 years ago. The league's first store, at 32 Main Street, sells crafts and produce, from pottery to jam. Across the street, the Corner House Inn (tel: 603-284 6219) is good for lunch, dinner, or an overnight stay.

Take Route 109 southward for 4 miles

Right: offering a warm New Hampshire welcome

(6km) to **Moultonborough,** where the **Old Country Store** has been selling necessities since it was built as a stagecoach stop in 1781. Now one of the oldest continually operating stores in the country, the venerable emporium is particularly good for local cheeses and maple products. Its museum features old-time tools, as well as a Concord Coach. Made in Concord, New Hampshire, these vehicles, traditionally associated with the Wild West, would stop outside the store front.

Fantasy Mansion

You will find a mansion known as the **Castle in the Clouds** (Route 171; tel: 1-800 729 2468) 3 miles (5km) from Moultonborough via routes 109 and 171. This remarkable edifice recalls the days when millionaires really knew how to express their wealth through opulent architectural statements. Shoe manufacturer Thomas G Plant started to build this fantasy 16-room retirement home in 1911, on a lofty site overlooking the Ossipee Mountains. The Castle in the Clouds is constructed of locally-quarried granite, and was originally surrounded by a 6,300-acre (2,550 ha) estate. In addition to touring the castle and grounds, you can rent horses for a one-hour guided trail ride, and take a tram for a tour of the Castlesprings water bottling facility and Lucknow microbrewery. Plant lived here for more than 30 years before dying poor after a string of ill-advised investments.

Head back onto Route 109 for the 17-mile (27km) drive along the Lake Winnipesaukee shore south to Wolfeboro.

10. THE WHITE MOUNTAINS *(see map, p58)*

A one- or two-day drive through New Hampshire's loftiest mountains, taking in Mt Washington – New England's highest point.

Follow Route 112 (the scenic Kancamagus Highway) west from Conway; head north on Route 3 and I-93 and east on Route 302. Go north via Route 16 to routes 2 and 115, for a northerly loop that links back with Route 302.

Once the rugged frontier of New England, New Hampshire's White Mountains emerged as a tourist playground in the days of railroad travel and grand hotels. Today the 800,000-acre (325,000 ha) White Mountain National Forest offers miles of unspoiled vistas, primitive terrain, and modern recreational facilities.

From Conway, set out on the 37-mile (60km) **Kancamagus Highway** (Route 112). Branching west through forested mountains, the road constitutes one of New England's great scenic experiences. After cresting at Kancamagus Pass, the highway descends to join Route 3 at Lincoln. If you're not averse to entertainment

Left: the Flume chasm

featuring trained animals, check out **Clark's Trading Post** (tel: 603-745 8913), where the attractions include bear shows. On leaving Lincoln, follow Route 3 and I-93 25 miles (40km) north to Bethlehem.

Several of New Hampshire's most famous natural wonders line Route 3 and I-93 in **Franconia Notch**, one of three passes through the mountains. The **Flume** (May–Oct daily 9am–5pm) is an 800-ft (250-meter) glacially-carved chasm through which a walkway follows a rushing stream and a chain of waterfalls. A few miles ahead, the **Old Man of the Mountains** looms high above the notch. This natural rock face has become the symbol of New Hampshire, and appears on the state's US quarter coin. To reach the peak of Franconia Notch, take the **Cannon Mountain Aerial Tramway** (I-93, exits 2 & 3; tel: 603-823 8800), a cable-suspended lift that serves the Cannon Mountain ski area. Not far from the tramway base, it's always winter at the **New England Ski Museum** (daily noon–5pm; tel: 603-823 7177), where photos and antique equipment chart the development of local skiing.

The **Frost Place** (tel: 603-823 5510) on Franconia's Ridge Road, was once farmed by Robert Frost (1874–1963); the rural scenes and plain speech of upcountry Yankeedom inspired him to write some of America's greatest poetry. There is a Frost museum at the house, and a nature trail on the grounds.

Pollen-free Bethlehem

Bethlehem has long been famous as a resort town, especially with allergy sufferers, who benefit from its pollen-free environment. Popular today with golfers – it has two fine courses – Bethlehem is a good stopover option. The Adair Inn (80 Guider Lane; tel: 603-444 2600) with its Tim-bir Alley restaurant (tel: 603-444 6142) is recommended.

On leaving Bethlehem, follow Route 302 east: you will see the White Mountains' peaks huddled together to the north and south. Passing Twin Mountain, the road moves southward, rising toward the heights of Crawford Notch. This central mountain pass is 19 miles (31km) from Bethlehem. Just north of the notch's crest, two venerable institutions date back to an era of

Above: the way to travel in Franconia Notch State Park

spectacular engineering and construction feats. The coal-fired steam locomotives of the **Mt Washington Cog Railway** (tel: 603-278 5404), completed in 1869, haul passengers up gradients so steep they are almost sheer to the 6,300ft (1,900-meter) peak. At the **Sherman Adams Summit Building** (tel: 603-466-3988) at the peak, you might want to visit the museum. This fascinating institution presents a history of weather – the world's highest wind speed of 231mph (372kph) was recorded right here in 1936.

The **Mt Washington Hotel** (Route 302; tel: 603-278 1000) stands at the foot of the mountain, just south of the railway's base station. Celebrating its centennial in 2002, the Mt Washington is the last of the region's grand hotels

that once catered to clients who arrived by rail and stayed all summer. Now splendidly restored and open all year, this great wedding cake of a building is ideal for skiers, golfers, and hikers.

A Tourism Capital

North Conway is a bargain-hunter's paradise. Pass the crest of Crawford Notch, follow Route 302 for 26 miles (42km) to this, the capital of White Mountains tourism. En route, in Harts Location, you might stop at the cozy Notchland Inn (tel: 603-374 6131) in a stone-and-timber mansion. Escaping the hubbub of North Conway traffic, ride on the **Conway Scenic Railroad** (tel: 603-356 5251), departing from a Victorian station in downtown North Conway. Or head north to **Glen** (Route 16 for 9 miles/14km) for a quiet night and fine cuisine at the Bernerhof (Route 302; tel: 603-383 9132). The Red Parka Pub (on the same road) also does good food.

Just north of Glen, **Story Land** (Route 16; mid-June–Labor Day: daily; weekends through Columbus Day) offers children's shows and 16 rides in a storybook-theme setting. The nearby **Heritage New Hampshire** (mid-June–mid-Oct daily), presents a history of the state through hands-on exhibits.

For the northern spur of this itinerary, continue on Route 16 for 10 miles (16km) to **Pinkham Notch**, the easternmost pass. Here the **Appalachian Mountain Club** (tel: 603-466 2727) offers bunk-style and private accommodations. Trails from the club's Information Center lead to the summit of Mt Washington. Club personnel should be able to advise you of weather and trail conditions. Just 5 miles (8km) to the north of Pinkham is the base station for the **Mt Washington Auto Road** (tel: 603-466 3988). The gradients of this 8-mile (13km) toll route to the summit reach an extremely steep 18 degrees. Always thrilling, the road is a veritable highway to the clouds – and to magnificent views when they disperse.

Unless you're returning directly to North Conway via Route 16, finish the drive by heading north to Gorham (8 miles/13km past the Auto Road). Follow Route 2 west for 19 miles (31km) to Route 302 at Twin Mountain. From here, it's a 12-mile (19km) drive west to north–south I-93.

Above: a Mt Washington Cog Railway coal-fired steam locomotive

11. THE MAINE COAST *(see maps, below & p64)*

Follow the Maine coast 'Down East' from Portland, the state's largest city and cultural center, to the rugged parklands and resort town of Bar Harbor on Mt Desert Island. En route, the villages of Maine's ragged coastline, and a scattering of unspoiled islands, make for wonderful side trips. Allow three days, or more if you want to visit the islands.

From Portland, follow Route 1 north. Route 15 is the main highway to the Blue Hill peninsula; access to Bar Harbor and Acadia National Park is via Route 3.

A map of Maine suggests that you are driving 'up' east (and north), not 'Down East' as the locals say. The term is a throwback to Portland's heyday, when southern New England relied on lumber shipped from Maine's busy wharves. This rocky coast is still imbued with the flavor of the sea: along Route 1 and its side roads, you are never far from a 'lobster pound' that sells the crustaceans to eat on the spot, or boiled to go.

Longfellow's Childhood

The 60-mile (96km) stretch of Maine coast south of Portland has lots of attractive features; the towns of York, Ogunquit, Wells, and Kennebunkport all enjoy fine beaches, and Old Orchard Beach is a lively, old-fashioned resort. But it is north of **Portland** that Maine's character asserts itself most clearly. Portland's most famous son, Henry Wadsworth Longfellow (1807–82), grew up during the city's

Above: beer is brewed on the premises

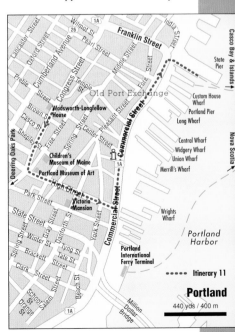

golden era, and his memory is preserved at the 1785 **Wadsworth Longfellow House** (489 Congress Street; June–Oct daily 10am–4pm; tel: 207-979 0427). This, his childhood home and Portland's oldest brick house, is packed with original furnishings. Farther along Congress Street, at 7 Congress Square, the **Portland Museum of Art** (10am–5pm; tel: 207-775 6148) displays works by American artists such as Edward Hopper, Andrew Wyeth, and Winslow Homer, as well as a good collection of European paintings by Degas, Picasso, and Monet.

The **Victoria Mansion** (109 Danforth Street; tel: 207-772 4841) is one of America's most extravagant Victorian homes. Built in 1859, its sedate brownstone facade belies a riotously ornate interior.

Cruise Around the Calendar Islands

Portland owes much of its present-day distinction to the transformation of its dilapidated waterfront district into the **Old Port Exchange** (Fore, Middle, Market, and Exchange streets). This neighborhood is full of bookstores, antique and crafts shops, boutiques, and cafes. For beer brewed on the premises, you can try Gritty McDuff's pub (396 Fore Street). Alternatively, visit **Deering Oaks Park** (State Street and Park Avenue). Designed by Frederick Law Olmstead, it is an ideal place for a stroll. The air is even fresher on a **Casco Bay Lines** cruise (Maine State Pier; tel: 207-774 7871)

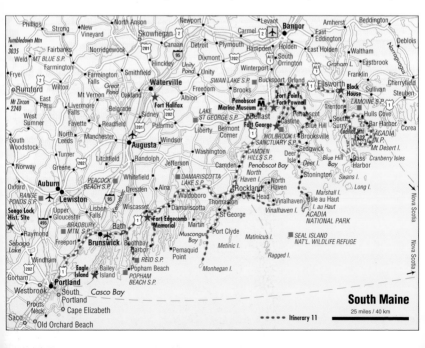

South Maine

25 miles / 40 km

••••• Itinerary 11

itineraries

around the bay's Calendar islands, so named because there are 365 of them.

Head north out of Portland on Route 1 for the 17-mile (27km) drive to **Freeport**, New England's most famous outlet-mall (discounted brand-name goods) town. The numerous outlet stores *(see Shopping, page 70)* that line Freeport's streets arrived in the wake of **L.L. Bean** (95 Main Street). Founded in 1912 by Leon Leonwood Bean as a purveyor of the waterproof hunting boots that are still a mainstay, Bean sells just about everything related to the outdoor life, especially items with the American-country-gentry look.

Brunswick, 10 miles (16km) north along this busy stretch of Route 1, is the home of prestigious **Bowdoin College**. Two Bowdoin alumni, the explorers Admiral Robert E. Peary and Captain Donald MacMillan, are remembered at the **Peary-MacMillan Arctic Museum** (Hubbard Hall; Tues–Sat 10am–5pm, Sun 2pm–5pm; tel: 207-725 3416). Here you will find photos, documents, and equipment from their polar expeditions. The Bowdoin **Museum of Art** (Walker Building; Tues–Sat 10am–5pm, Sun 2–5pm; tel: 207-725 3275) exhibits works by American colonial, Impressionist, and modern painters, and paintings by European masters.

The next stop, farther north on Route 1, is the shipbuilding town of **Bath**, where US naval vessels are still constructed. The **Maine Maritime Museum and Shipyard** (243 Washington Street; daily 9.30am–5pm; tel: 207-443 1316) chronicles the industry of a former era. The fishing schooner *Sherman Zwicker* is a big attraction here, but it is not always in port. For a more direct taste of the sea, turn south onto Route 127 just beyond Bath for **Reid State Park**, where 1½ miles (2km) of beaches face protected bay waters.

Windjammer Days

Numerous visitors are attracted by the diverse charms of **Wiscasset** (9 miles/14km north of Bath along Route 1), in particular its elegant, Federal-style homes and numerous antique shops. But be warned that traffic can get a bit thick here in summer. An even more popular destination is **Boothbay Harbor** (10 miles/16km south of Wiscasset), whose narrow streets and quay-side stores are those of the quintessential Maine fishing village. The scene is at its most picturesque when sailing vessels convene in the harbor, as they do during Windjammer Days every June *(see Calendar of Events, page 79)*. If you plan to be here at this time of year, book your accommodations in advance. The Kenniston Hill Inn, set in a 200-year-old home, is a good option.

You can take to the seas yourself on a lovely wooden windjammer at **Rockland** (42 miles/68km north of Wiscasset via Route 1). The schooners *Heritage* (tel: 1-800 648 4544 or, from outside Maine, 1-800 542 5030) and *Victory Chimes* (tel: 207-594 0755; or 1-800 745 5651) are among several that sail out of Rockland harbor on three-and six-day coastal cruise. Rock-

Above Left: relaxing in the evening shadows after a hard day at work, and school
Right: Wiscasset captures the atmosphere of a bygone age

land's **Farnsworth Art Museum** (356 Main
Street; 9am–5pm; tel: 207-596 6457) has an
excellent American collection, and is strong on
paintings by the Wyeth family, which was associated with Maine. Visit the **Owls Head Transportation Museum** (Route 73; 10am–5pm;
tel: 207-594 4418) to see antique cars and air-
planes, and weekend air shows. Waterworks
(Lindsey Street, off Main Street) is a good spot
for lunch and a Maine microbrew.

This is Maine island country. The *Laura B.*
(tel: 207-372 8848) sails from Port Clyde
(10 miles/16km south of Rockland via
Route 73) for **Monhegan**, which is some
10 miles/16km offshore. The island, which
features 17 miles (27km) of crisscrossing
hiking trails, has long been a favorite of
painters inspired by its windswept countryside
and fishing village. From Owls Head, you can
sail on the Maine State ferry (tel: 207-696-2202) to **Vinalhaven** and **North
Haven**, both serene islands with tidy villages overlooking Penobscot Bay.

The town of **Camden**, 8 miles (13km) north of Rockland on Route 1,
enjoys a spectacular location on the bay, and its snowy white captains'
mansions attest to its seafaring prosperity. One of these, tucked among
downtown's stores and galleries, is the Camden Maine Stay
(22 High Street; tel: 207-236 0621), a snug inn dating to 1802.
For the best panoramic view of Camden and surrounding
waters, head for **Camden Hills State Park**, just to the north
of town, and hike or drive to the summit of the 800 ft (250-
meter) **Mt Battie**.

Continue north on coast-hugging Route 1 for 39 miles (63km)
to Orland, then head south for 14 miles (23km) via Route 175
to **Castine**, perched on a peninsula near the head of Penobscot
Bay. The ruins of **Fort George** are a reminder of a tumultuous
past – the British occupied Castine during the Revolution. Today
the Maine Maritime Academy trains merchant seamen here. The town constitutes a collection of Federal and Greek Revival structures, many given
over to stores and taverns. The Castine Inn (Main Street; tel: 207-326 4365)
has a formal garden and an innovative restaurant.

Blue Hill Potteries

The 20 mile- (32km-) long **Blue Hill peninsula** forms the eastern bulwark
of Penobscot Bay. Unfortunately the peninsula's street plan involves the most
confusing tangle of roads in New England. And the rolling terrain of woods
and meadows doesn't make directions any simpler. The main road, Route 15,
heads south from Route 1 near Orland. You might decide to stop at the town
of **Blue Hill**, which is known for its potteries. Of these, **Rowantrees** (Union
Street; tel: 207-374 5535) was inspired by Mahatma Gandhi to use local

Above: strolling through the woods of Mt Desert Island
Right: a Vinalhaven fishing boat joins the quest for lobsters

itineraries

mineral glazes as the basis for a crafts enterprise. Farther south on the peninsula, a causeway leads to the fishing village of Stonington on Deer Isle, from which you can take a ferry (tel: 207-367 5193) to tranquil **Isle au Haut**. Rugged and unspoiled, this island lies partly within the Acadia National Park.

The East Coast's Highest Point
One of the most-visited parks in the country, **Acadia National Park** (for park information, tel: 207-288 3338) covers much of **Mount Desert Island** (accessible via causeway from Route 1 via Route 3 at Ellsworth, 20 miles/32km east of Orland). The park constitutes the perfect distillation of the Maine coast – stark granite headlands, upland meadows, deep pine forests, and thundering surf, all crowned by the **Cadillac Mountain** which, at 1,530 ft (465 meters), is the highest point on the East Coast. The mountain is celebrated as the first place in the nation to greet the morning rays of the sun, an event welcomed each day by hikers and motorists who make the trip to the rocky summit – a place of sweeping, dramatic views at any time of day.

Most of the development on Mt Desert Island is focused in and around **Bar Harbor**, a 19th-century resort facing Frenchmans Bay. In 1947 a fire destroyed the Rockefeller mansion and other grand residences. (Much of the parkland was bequested by John D Rockefeller Jr, who was responsible for the island's lovely carriage roads.) The resort attracts an upscale sailing crowd. Bar Harbor is a good base for a number of activities: you can tour the island's smaller villages; drive along Acadia's 27-mile (43km) Loop Road, which connects beaches and seaside vantage points; or stroll among scores of boutiques and bistros. Miramonte (69 Mount Desert Street; tel: 207-288 4263) is a good place to stay; of the many local restaurants, which seem to serve lobster with everything, try George's (7 Stephen's Lane; tel: 207-288 4505).To return to Portland and points south, head inland to Bangor, 28 miles (45km) north via Alternate Route 1, and pick up I-95 south.

Leisure
Activities

SHOPPING

Big-city and suburban mall shopping in New England has developed in much the same way as in the rest of the US – you won't have to look far for a Banana Republic or a Gap if you run low on khakis. The region also takes pride in several time-honored local retail traditions, such as antiques and crafts. A recent development is the 'factory outlet' phenomenon: scores of stores, clustered together, offer bargains on merchandise for which you would pay top dollar in most malls and downtown locations.

For regular shopping, **Boston** has the region's best array of choices. The city's major retail districts include downtown's Washington Street, where **Macy's** and **Filene's** (and the chaotic, deep-discounting **Filene's Basement**) are the big names. Also good is the **Back Bay**, with its **Newbury Street** couturiers and upscale **Prudential Center** and **Copley Place** shops (**Lord & Taylor; Nieman-Marcus**). **Faneuil Hall Marketplace** features dozens of specialty boutiques in restored historic buildings.

Antiques

New England is the spiritual home of the American antiques business. Having been settled for nearly 400 years, it was the first part of the country to realize that a fortune was hidden in its attics. Until well into the 20th century, only European antiques had any real value. Since then dealers have prospered on the profits made from fine 17th- and 18th-century American furniture – much of it fashioned by master craftsmen in Boston, Newport, and Portsmouth – that they bought for a pittance. New England's attics have largely run dry, but there are plenty of finds to be had, as the region's dealers import stock from all over the world.

In New England, antiques dealers tend to stick together. In Boston, some of the most distinguished are around **Charles Street**.

Specialties of the district include high-end furniture, porcelain and silver, and marine paintings (although most of the city's better art dealers are on **Newbury Street** in the Back Bay). For less expensive items, try Charles Street's **Boston Antique Co-op**.

Outside the city, eastern Massachusetts's biggest concentration of dealers is in the North Shore town of **Essex**, where at least a score of shops specialize in everything from fine English furniture, to 18th-century New England pieces, to old maps, to the bizarre and funky. Out on Cape Cod, in **Provincetown**, dealers tend to favor camp and kitsch items from the mid-20th century.

Several times each summer, the western Massachusetts town of **Brimfield** hosts New England's biggest antiques event: hundreds of dealers converge to trade with each other, and sell their wares to the public. Heading north, the Vermont town of **Newfane** has a fine concentration of antique shops, while down in Connecticut the towns of **Putnam**, **New Preston**, and **Old Saybrook** have all attracted a phalanx of dealers.

Crafts

New England's tradition of fine craftsmanship dates back to colonial times, when things were hand-made by necessity. More

Left: Faneuil Hall area in the summer
Right: textiles for sale, Center Sandwich

recently, the region has attracted artisans who want to live and work in a place where they can absorb inspiration from the past – and find a ready market among quality-conscious locals and visitors. Dedicated craftspeople help sustain New England's reputation as a place that honors function, aesthetics, and honest workmanship.

The **League of New Hampshire Craftsmen** is an association of Granite State artisans – potters, jewelers, woodworkers, glass blowers, weavers – who sell their work at six state locations, including the league's place of origin, **Center Sandwich**. Similarly, the **Vermont State Craft Center at Frog Hollow**, with locations in Middlebury and Burlington, selects the best work by Vermont artisans. Count on finding just about anything hand-made, from an Adirondack-style bedroom set to a rosewood-framed looking glass to landscapes by Vermont printmakers. For prints and furniture in Vermont, the **Stephen Huneck Gallery** in Woodstock has whimsical designs based on animals, while the **Warren Kimble Gallery** in Brandon is good for contemporary folk art.

Vermont is home to chunky **Bennington Pottery**, available at galleries in Bennington and Burlington. Another great pottery tradition lives on in Blue Hill, Maine, where **Rowantrees Pottery** and other makers use locally-mined minerals to create vivid glazes.

Fine glassware is associated with **Sandwich** on Cape Cod. The town has a fine museum of locally-made glass, and you can buy today's products – and watch them being hand-blown – at the **Pairpoint Crystal Company** in nearby **Sagamore**. Handcrafted glass is the centerpiece of the elegant complex of water-powered workrooms, shop, and restaurant at **Simon Pearce** in Quechee, Vermont.

The **lightship basket**, a New England handicraft, is a specialty of **Nantucket**. The densely woven wicker baskets hark back to long, lonely tours of duty on old-time lightships (ships used as floating lighthouses), and are sold today as women's purses, complete with faux-scrimshaw inserts. They take a long time to make, and don't come cheap.

Wine

Winemaking is relatively new to the region. In the past few decades, enthusiasts have discovered that much of the area's soils and microclimate are suited to viniculture. Established vineyards include **Sakonnet** in **Little Compton** (Rhode Island) and **Chicama** on **Martha's Vineyard**. In northwestern Connecticut, Hopkins and Haight are two respected vineyards, and even frosty Vermont has **Snow Farm** in **South Hero**, on the relatively mild Champlain Islands.

Factory Outlets

The factory-outlet phenomenon in New England has two points of origin. One was the availability of inexpensive floor space in once-thriving mills. This provided the spur in the old factory city of **Fall River**, Massachusetts, which became known for producing clothes such as sweaters. The other factor was the influence of outdoor equipment and clothing supplier **L L Bean**, whose 24-hour-a-day location in **Freeport**, Maine, drew so many visitors that other retailers moved in for a share of the market. Today scores of top-name purveyors of men's and women's clothing, shoes, housewares, and gifts have set up shop in downtown Freeport, where you can find bargains on overstock, last-season, and second-quality items. The formula has been adopted in **North Conway**, New Hampshire; **Manchester**, Vermont; **Kittery**, Maine; **Wrentham**, Massachusetts; and **Clinton**, Connecticut.

Specialty Shopping

Some New England specialty stores have become destinations in themselves. **Orvis** in Manchester has a country-chic persona built around its line of exquisite hand-made fly rods and fishing tackle. In Maine, **Kittery Trading Post** will outfit an expedition into the North Woods with nearly as much panache as at L L Bean himself. Also in Maine, **Old Town Canoes** is recommended for its sleek vessels, real and models alike. **Yankee Candle** in Deerfield is a vast emporium of candles and gifts, complete with Bavarian and Victorian theme rooms. **Peter Limmer and Sons** in Intervale, New Hampshire, make the country's finest hiking boots. The array of goods at **Vermont Country Store** in Weston includes woolen hunting pants, local cheddar cheese, manual typewriters, crystallized ginger, and tea cozies.

EATING OUT

For several generations, the expression 'New England cuisine' could be taken two ways: to traditionalists, it signified something that was comfortably predictable; to gourmets, it was a contradiction in terms.

The culinary tradition of New England synthesizes old English cookery techniques with the ingredients that were available in the colonies. A dish such as New England boiled dinner – beef brisket poached with root vegetables and cabbage – might easily have graced an English table 300 years ago. As far as the local additions are concerned, early New Englanders could dip into an immense natural larder bursting with game, fish and shellfish, native berries, and that great gift of the Indians, corn (maize).

Traditional Standbys

Today's visitors to the region will have no trouble finding old standbys, such as Yankee pot roast (similar to the boiled dinner, but made with round roast and a thickened gravy), creamy clam or fish chowder, and Indian pudding. The pudding, a baked corn porridge affair, is usually served – as it definitely wasn't during colonial times – with vanilla ice cream. But these time-honored dishes have largely been relegated to the menus of restaurants that make a specialty of them, and of 'ye olde' colonial decor too.

New England has long since joined the trend toward a cuisine greatly influenced by new European and Asian concepts of super-fresh ingredients, lighter stocks and sauces, and a contrast of flavors and textures. There is, moreover, the element of authentic ethnic dining: most cities and college towns offer Szechuan, Thai, northern Italian, Middle Eastern, Indian, Japanese, Korean, African, and Caribbean cuisines.

Seafood

New England's seafood tradition is not to be confused with that of other American coastal regions such as Louisiana or the Pacific Northwest. Fried clams, for instance, are nowhere better than along the North Shore of Massachusetts. A drive along the Maine coast can become a moveable feast of lobster: boiled and served roadside 'in the rough,' in rolls bulging with sweet meat cubed or shredded with mayonnaise or melted butter, or in rich bisques and stews. Wellfleet oysters, Chatham scallops from Cape Cod, fresh-caught swordfish and bluefish are all considered to be among the world's greatest saltwater treats.

When it comes to culinary oddities and idiosyncracies, New England certainly has its share. All of the following can be found in the region: French Canadian-style breakfasts, with baked beans crowding eggs and sausages; clam pizza in Connecticut; the vinegar-marinated Portuguese pork and seafood dishes that are especially common

in southeastern Massachusetts; and muffins (or pancakes) filled with local blueberries, which can frequently be purchased from roadside outlets in Maine.

If it's fast food you're after, this is the place for giving the chain eateries a miss, and heading for a diner instead. This is because the diner phenomenon was born in Providence, Rhode Island, and matured in Worcester, Massachusetts. Slide into a booth, open the pages of the Boston *Globe*, order a cup of coffee, and ask the waitress if they make their own pies.

The following is a rough price guide for a three-course dinner, excluding beverages, tax and a tip. Bear in mind that lunch menus are frequently less expensive.

$ = under $15
$$ = $15–$25
$$$ = $25–$40
$$$$ = over $40

Above: Wellfleet oysters – one of the world's great saltwater treats

Connecticut
Café Routier
1080 Boston Post Road, Old Saybrook
Tel: 860-388 6270
Artfully-prepared French and American dishes, a fine wine list, and candlelit tables in white linen tablecloths all contribute to this restaurant's fine reputation. $$

Copper Beech Inn
46 Main Street, Ivoryton
Tel: 860-767 0330
Country French cuisine served in the candlelit dining room of a romantic inn. Try the house specialty bouillabaisse. Reservations essential; jackets and ties for men. $$–$$$$

Louis' Lunch
263 Crown Street, New Haven
Tel: 203-562 5507
This National Register of Historic Places luncheonette is the birthplace of the hamburger, which is still served up with a slice of tomato or cheese on toast. $

Mystic Pizza
56 West Main Street, Mystic
Tel: 860-536 3700
Pizza parlor that Julia Roberts put on the map: fine pizza, subs, and Italian entrees. $

Maine
George's
7 Stephen's Lane, Bar Harbor
Tel: 288 4505
Fine linen and fresh flowers set the mood for elegant, intimate dining with Mediterranean flair. Prix-fixe menu, and live jazz in season. $$$

Gritty McDuff's
396 Fore Street, Portland
Tel: 207-772 2739
Portland's original brew pub serves its own fine ales along with both typical British pub fare and local seafood dishes. $$

Street and Co.
33 Wharf Street, Portland
Tel: 207-775 0887
Seafood reigns – fresh, tasty, and piping hot. Treatments range from simple steamed clams to lobster *fra diavolo*. $$–$$$

Waterworks
Lindsey Street, Rockland
Tel: 207-596 2753
Local microbrews and single-malt Scotches; hearty, down-home American fare. $–$$

Massachusetts
Boston/Cambridge
Legal Seafoods
Prudential Center, 800 Boylston Street (Back Bay), Boston; tel: 617-266 6800
Copley Place, 100 Huntington Ave (Back Bay), Boston; tel: 617-266 7775
26 Park Plaza (Back Bay) Boston; tel: 617-426 4444
255 State Street (Waterfront), Boston; tel: 617-227 3115
Fine chain serving food with an Asian influence. No reservations; long waits. $$–$$$$

Locke-Ober Café
3 Winter Place (Downtown), Boston
Tel: 617-542 1340
Has a gentleman's-club ambience. Outstanding wine list. Jacket and tie. Reservations essential. Closed Sun. $$$$

Mamma Maria
3 North Square, Boston
Tel: 617-523 0007
Romantic brownstone situated in the North End; fine Italian food. Reservations essential. $$$$

Elsewhere in Massachusetts
Antonio's
267 Coggeshall Street, New Bedford
Tel: 508-990 3636
Portuguese dishes, such as *bacalau* (salt cod), pork and shellfish stew, in a friendly eatery. $–$$

Chillingsworth
2449 Main Street, Route 6A, Brewster
Tel: 508-896 3640
Classic French cuisine and great wine cellar. Also a less expensive bistro menu. $$$$

The Grog
13 Middle Street, Newburyport
Tel: 978-465 8008
Pub fare, light meals, and live entertainment. The Grog burger is a standout. $–$$

Right: a classic New England lobster dinner

Helsinki Tea Company
284 Main Street, Great Barrington
Tel: 413-528 3394
Big portions of well-seasoned dishes inspired by Russia and Finland in a setting of pillows and fringed curtains. $–$$

Portside Chowder House
Bearskin Neck, Rockport
Tel: 978-546 7045
Fish chowder and a platter of steamers; also hamburgers, soups, salads. $–$$

Scandia
25 State Street, Newburyport
Tel: 978-462 6271
Popular for a night out: continental fare well-prepared and elegantly served in a candlelit dining room on the main street. $$$

Trattoria Il Vesuvio
242 Pittsfield Road, Lenox
Tel: 413-637 4904
Dishes prepared from scratch: *arrosto de vitello* (roast breast of veal stuffed with sliced prosciutto and spinach) is outstanding, as is homemade *tiramisu.* $$–$$$

Truc Orient Express
3 Harris Street, West Stockbridge
Tel: 413-232 4204
Creative dishes ('Happy Pancake,' 'Shaking Beef') are elegantly presented in this upscale Vietnamese restaurant. $–$$

White Rainbow
65 Main Street, Gloucester
Tel: 978-281 0017
Candlelit dining, fine New American fare (prime beef, fresh fish). Closed Mon. $$$

Woodman's of Essex
121 Main Street, Route 133, Essex
Tel: 978-768 6451
Fried clams were 'invented' at this in-the-rough restaurant overlooking the mud flats. Also lobsters, chowder, and a raw bar. $–$$

New Hampshire

The 1785 Inn
Route 16, Intervale
Tel: 603-356 9025
Award-winning restaurant/inn with a huge fireplace and Colonial atmosphere has an extensive list of appetizers, creative continental entrees, and a superb wine list. $$$

Kona Mansion
Moultonborough Neck Rd, Moultonborough
Tel: 603-253 4900
Creative contemporary fare – baked stuffed shrimp and grilled steak – in Victorian dining rooms of an elegant mansion overlooking Lake Winnepesaukee. $$–$$$

The Library
401 State Street, Portsmouth
Tel: 603-431 5202
Intimate, upscale dining in former Rockingham Hotel. The menu stresses traditional favorites; after dinner, enjoy a cigar in the English-style pub downstairs. $$–$$$

The Red Parka Pub
Route 302, Glen
Tel: 383 4344
Even when there's no snow, this informal, aprés-ski pub/restaurant is one of the hottest spots in town. Hand-cut steaks and barbecued ribs are among the house specialties, as is the salad bar. $–$$

Shibley's
On the Pier, Alton Bay
Tel: 603-875 3636
Try a seafood platter on the deck overlooking the bay, or the seafood shack/ice cream stand for lighter, less formal fare. $–$$

Rhode Island

Blue Grotto Restaurant
210 Atwells Avenue, Providence
401-272 9030
Excellent fried calamari, spinach ravioli, or *bistecca fiorentina* at this mainstay of the Federal Hill Italian neighborhood. $$–$$$

The Black Pearl
Bannister's Wharf, Newport
Tel: 401-846 5264
Yachting types flock here. There's a casual inn and formal dining (jackets required), with French and American fare. $$$$

The Mooring
Sayer's Wharf, Newport
Tel: 401-846 2260
Award-winning seafood chowder and a fine selection of fish dishes at a family restaurant overlooking the harbor. $$–$$$

Olympia Tea Room
30 Bay Street, Watch Hill
Tel: 401-348 8211
Tiny restaurant that has hardly changed since 1916. Try stuffed quahogs, and Avondale swan — an ice cream concoction with whipped cream, chocolate sauce, and puff pastry. Closed Nov–Mar. $$–$$$

Vermont

Beansie's Bus
Battery Park, Burlington
Look for the converted yellow school bus at the waterfront: for years the Burlington landmark has been serving up great french fries, burgers, and hot dogs. $

Blue Moon Cafe
35 School Street, Stowe
Tel: 802-253 7006
Contemporary American cuisine in an elegant bistro, with house specialties such as seared Atlantic salmon with pepita crust and slow-cooked peppers. $$–$$$

Bryant House
Weston Village
Tel: 824-6287
New England favorites (chicken pot pie) in a Victorian setting. Lunch only.

The Common Ground
25 Elliot Street, Brattleboro
Tel: 802-257 0855
Enduring cooperative housed in a renovated warehouse; good selection of vegetarian, fish, and poultry dishes, sugar-free desserts. $

Fire & Ice
26 Seymour Street, Middlebury
Tel: 802-388 7166
Prime steaks, chicken, the house special mashed potatoes, and a fine salad bar. $$

Leunig's Bistro
Church and College streets, Burlington
Tel: 802-863 3759
Creative continental fare, great live and recorded music, and sidewalk seating: *the* place to dine on a fine summer's day. $–$$

Pané é Saluté
61 Central Street, Woodstock
Tel: 802-457 4882
Tiny bakery that has grown into a full-scale restaurant. In addition to Italian regional breads, there are daily lunch and dinner specials, a fine selection of wines, and great homemade desserts. $–$$

Parima Thai Restaurant
185 Pearl Street, Burlington
Authentic dishes – curries, *pad thais*, and the house special crispy roasted duck in tamarind sauce – in handsome rooms. $–$$

Villa Tragara
Route 100, Waterbury
Tel: 802-244 5288
Italian fare (creative pasta dishes) in 1820s farmhouse overlooking the mountains. Good wine menu. Closed Mon. $$–$$$

Woody's
Five Bakery Lane, Middlebury
Tel: 802-388 4182
Try Cajun shrimp, local lamb, or Caesar salad. Situated over Otter Creek. $$–$$$

nightlife

NIGHTLIFE

Given Boston's reputation as a bastion of high culture, and the presence in the region of so many institutions of higher learning, it's no wonder that New England is, after New York City, the nation's leader in serious music, theater, and dance. It is also big on popular-entertainment venues.

The **Boston Symphony** plays in season at Symphony Hall (301 Massachusetts Avenue, Boston; tel: 617-266 1492 or 1-800 274 8499), and at the **Tanglewood Music Festival** in the Berkshires *(see page 79)*. Also in summer, BSO musicians appear as the **Boston Pops** at Symphony Hall and in the Hatch Shell on Boston's Charles River Esplanade.

Elsewhere, the region's top cultural offerings tend to cluster in college towns and large cities. Connecticut's **Hartford Symphony** (tel: 860-244 2999), Maine's **Portland Symphony Orchestra** (tel: 207-77 8191), the **Vermont Symphony Orchestra** (tel: 802-864 5741), and the **Rhode Island Philharmonic** (tel: 401-831 3123) perform at home and road venues in their respective states.

All of the larger colleges and universities present performing arts series; contact state tourism agencies *(see Practical Information, page 83)* or individual college publicity offices for details.

On the pop front, lots of clubs and dives host aspiring singers and bands on Friday nights. The region draws tours by everyone from Joan Baez to Phish.

Nightclubs; Live Music and Comedy Clubs

Atlantic House
6 Masonic Place, Provincetown, MA
Tel: 508-487 3821
Popular gay gathering place. Dance bar; leather bar; Friday night theme parties.

Axis
13 Landsdown Street, Boston, MA
Tel: 617-262 2437
High-energy, club peaks on Saturday night with contemporary dance downstairs and new wave upstairs. Wear creative dress.

Blackburn Tavern Pub
267 East Main Street, Gloucester, MA
Tel: 978-282 4099
Live music on weekends and Sun brunch.

The Call
15 Elbow Street, Providence, RI
Tel: 401 751 2255
Showcase for the area's best blues bands.

Chaps
100 Warrenton Street, Boston, MA
Tel: 617-695 9500
Huge, flashy disco; long a popular gay spot, but also draws a large straight crowd. Traditional Sunday tea dance (6–10pm).

Chaser's
293 Commercial Street, Provincetown, MA
Tel: 508-487 7200
Popular lesbian nightspot features pool tables, dancing, and entertainment.

Above: New England provides plenty of opportunities to see top-class dance acts

The Chicken Box
16 Dave Street, Nantucket, MA
Tel: 508-228 9717
Rock bands every night in summer;
weekends rest of year.

Club Passim
47 Palmer Place, Cambridge, MA
Tel: 617-492 7679
The US's oldest folk club. Light fare
served during shows. No alcohol.

Comedy Zone
Radisson Hotel
60 Battery Street, Burlington, VT
Tel: 802-658 6500
Rising comedians are showcased in hotel
nightclub setting.

Fire & Water Coffee House
Old South Street, Northampton, MA
Tel: 413-586 8336
Live music and Wednesday night poetry
readings.

Foxwoods Resort Casino
Mashantucket Pequot Tribal Nation,
Mashantucket, CT
Tel: 860-396 6572
Vegas-quality headliners in a 1,400-seat
theater.

The Grog
13 Middle Street, Newburyport, MA
Tel: 978-465 8008
A local institution, offering blues, rock,
and folk performers several nights a week.

Hot Tin Roof
Martha's Vineyard Airport, Edgartown-
West Tisbury Road, West Tisbury
(Martha's Vineyard), MA
Tel: 508-693 1137
Singer Carly Simon owns this popular
nightspot, which hosts name pop bands.

The Iron Horse
10 Pearl Street, Northampton, MA
Tel: 413-584 0610
Live folk, jazz and comedy; dinner.

Nectar's
188 Main Street, Burlington, VT
Tel: 802-658 4771
The place that launched Phish; showcases
hot local groups; no cover charge.

Newport Blues Café
286 Thames Street, Newport, RI
Tel: 401-841 5510
Newport's best blues venue.

Nick's Comedy Shop
100 Warrenton Street, Boston, MA
Tel: 617-482 0930
Large venue with local comics nightly
(not Mon). Nightclub and restaurant.

Regattabar
Charles Hotel
1 Bennett Street, Cambridge, MA
Tel: 617-661 5000
Upscale bar, big names (not Sun, Mon).

Ri Ra
123 Church Street, Burlington, MA
Tel: 802-860 9401
Irish music in 'authentic' Dublin-pub
setting.

Roxy
Tremont Hotel
279 Tremont Street, Boston, MA
Tel: 617-337 7699
Grand live-music ballroom. Busy on
weekends with a well-dressed crowd.

Shannon Door Pub
Route 16, Jackson, NH
Tel: 603-383 4211
Restaurant/tavern; folk, blues, light rock.

Left: live action at a Boston blues bar

Wobbly Barn
Killington Road, Killington, VT
Tel: 802-422 3392
Ski-season joint for blues, rock, dancing.

Concerts, Theater, and Dance
Berkshire Performing Arts Center
70 Kemble Street, Lenox, MA
Tel: 413-637 1800
Name pop, classical, jazz; children's acts.

Boston Ballet
Wang Center
270 Tremont Sreet, Boston MA
Tel: 617-482 9393
Classical, new works by top ballet troupe.

Cabot Street Cinema Theater
268 Cabot Street, Beverly, MA
Tel: 978-927 3677
Magic show on Sunday in 750-seat theater.

Cape Cod Melody Tent
21 West Main Street, Hyannis, MA
Tel: 508-775 9100
Comedy and musicals in summer.

Charles Playhouse
74 Warrenton Street, Boston, MA
Tel: 617-426 5525
Blue Man Group performance-art.

Colonial Theatre
106 Boylston Street, Boston, MA
Tel: 617-426 9366
Ornate venue, big names, popular shows.

Fiynn Theatre for the Performing Arts
153 Main Street, Burlington, VT
Tel: 802-652 4500
Restored Art Deco building hosts Vermont Symphony, theater, big-name performers.

Goodspeed Opera House
Route 82, East Haddam, CT
Tel: 860-873 8668
Magnificent opera house presents plays and musicals (Apr–Dec). Tours in summer.

Jacob's Pillow Dance Festival
George Carter Road (Rte 20), Becket, MA
Tel: 413-637 1322; 413-243 0745 summer
Ballet and modern works.

Jordan Hall, New England Conservatory
30 Gainsborough Street, Boston MA
Tel: 617-536 2412
Prestigious music school hosts the Boston Phil; chamber music, guest orchestras.

The Lakes Summer Theater
Route 25, Meredith, NH
Tel: 603-279 9933 or 800-643 9993
The Lakes Region's premier rep theater.

Loeb Drama Center
64 Brattle Street, Cambridge, MA
Tel: 617-547 8300
Home of the American Repertory Theater, which presents classic and first-run drama.

Paramount Performing Arts Theater
1700 Main Street, Springfield, MA
Tel: 413-734 5874
Pop, rock, country; comedy; children's programs, in a restored, 1920s cinema.

Playhouse Dinner Theater
194 Main Street, Amesbury, MA
Tel: 978-388 9444
Classic dramas and musicals by resident troupe; the region's oldest dinner theater.

Portland Performing Arts Center
25A Forest Avenue, Portland, ME
Tel: 207-761 0591
Theater, dance and music, year-round.

Seacoast Repertory Theatre
125 Bow Street, Portsmouth, NH
Tel: 603-433 4472 or 800-639 7650
Year-round drama and musicals.

Shubert Theatre
265 Tremont Street, Boston, MA
Tel: 617-482 9393
Home to Boston Lyric Opera Company.

Weston Playhouse
Village Green, Route 100, Weston, VT
Tel: 802-824 5288
Broadway material summer–early fall.

Yale Repertory Theatre
Chapel and York streets, New Haven, CT
Tel: 203-432 1234
Quality classic, premiere performances.

CALENDAR OF EVENTS

January

Chinese New Year (variable), Boston, MA: Chinatown holds the nation's third-largest Chinese New Year celebrations with three weeks of colorful parades and fireworks (tel: 617-536 4100).

Jackson Winter Carnival (third week), Jackson, NH: Featuring skiing and snowboard races, ice-sculpture competition, colorful parade and bonfire, jazz breakfast buffet (tel: 603-383 9356).

February

Dartmouth Winter Carnival (mid-month), Hanover, NH: This perennial Ivy League favorite brings students and outsiders together for events such as alpine and cross-country ski races, ski jumping, an ice-sculpture competition, and partying (603-643-3115).

Mad River Valley Winter Carnival (mid-month), Warren, VT: Ski, snowboard, and dog-sled races, and fireworks at Sugarbush Ski Area (tel: 802-496 2409).

March

New England Spring Flower Show (mid-month), Boston: Seven days of the nation's oldest flower show at Bay Side Exposition Center (tel: 617-536 9280).

Sled Dog Races (early month), Rangeley, ME: More than 100 teams from across the northeast compete in one of the region' biggest sled dog events (tel: 207-864 5364)

St Patrick's Day Parade (Sun nearest to Mar 17), Boston, MA: The Irish community parades through South Boston; Irish dancing and music in and around Faneuil Hall.

April

Boston Marathon (third Mon), Boston, MA The world's oldest annual marathon attracts runners from all over the world: the finish is at Copley Square (tel: 617-236 1652).

Maple Festival (early month), St Albans, VT: A three-day celebration of Vermont's most famous product, including 'sugar on snow' booths where you can taste warmed maple syrup drizzled on snow; also arts and crafts, antiques (tel: 802-524 2444).

Patriots Day (third Mon), Lexington, MA: The opening battle of American Revolution is commemorated with a full-scale reenactment on Lexington Green (tel: 781-862 1450).

May

Dodge Dealers' Grand Prix (late month), Lakeville, CT: famed Limerock Park hosts North America's largest sports car race (tel: 1-800-RACE-LRP).

Above: the Head of the Charles Regatta is the world's premier rowing event

Shelburne Museum Lilac Festival (late May), Shelburne, VT: Over 90 different varieties of lilac bloom on the grounds of Vermont's premier museum of folk art (tel: 802-985 3334).

June

Boston Harborfest (starts fourth week): Concerts and historical reenactments on the waterfront (tel: 617-227 1528).

Discover Jazz Festival (early June) Burlington, VT: The entire 'Queen City' area is the venue for nine days of jazz concerts (tel: 802-863 5966).

International Festival of Arts and Ideas (last two weeks), New Haven, CT: Theater, dance, classical music and jazz, poetry readings, and interactive children's activities (tel: 203-498 1212).

Windjammer Days (late month), Boothbay Harbor, ME: Sailing vessels parade in the harbor. Fireworks, concerts, parades, and church suppers (tel: 207-633 2353).

July

Antique & Classic Boat Rendezvous (late month), Mystic, CT: Mystic Seaport hosts annual gathering of pre-1950s wooden sail and motor boats, capped by a Sunday boat parade (tel: 860-572 5315).

Independence Day (Fourth), Boston, MA: Reading of the Declaration of Independence at the Old State House; evening Boston Pops concert and fireworks at the Hatch Shell on the river. Many grab a place on the lawn in the early morning (tel: 617-266 1492).

Tanglewood Music Festival (late June through summer), Lenox, MA: Boston Symphony performs at its summer home: sit indoors or picnic under the stars on the lawn (tel: 413-637 5165 or 1-800-274 8499).

August

Brooklyn Fair (last week), Brooklyn, CT: The nation's oldest agricultural fair features livestock shows, ox and horse pulls, home and garden exhibits, and entertainment and rides (tel: 860-779 0012).

Newport JVC Jazz Festival (mid-month), Newport, RI: One of the world's most famous jazz festivals brings together veteran performers and today's rising talents (tel: 401-847 3700).

Portsmouth Blues Festival (third week of month), Portsmouth, NH: Strawbery Banke Museum hosts two days of blues concerts by aspiring local, and established national, musicians (tel: 603-433-1106).

September

Eastern States Exposition (last two weeks of month), West Springfield, MA: this is New England's biggest fall fair featuring farm exhibits, animals, state exibits, midway, circus troops, and top music stars (tel: 413-737 2443).

Rhode Island Heritage Festival (mid-month), Providence, RI: Thirty ethnic groups showcase their music, dance, foods, and crafts (tel: 401-222 2678).

October

Fall Festival (second week), Camden, ME: Nearly 100 artists and artisans display their work outdoors in this handsome old seaport (tel: 207-236 4404).

Head of the Charles Regatta (penultimate Sun), Boston/Cambridge, MA: Crews from assorted points around the globe compete in the world's largest rowing event (tel: 617-864 8415).

November

Christmas at Blithewold (late Nov–Dec), Bristol, RI: Nightly concerts held in a gorgeously decorated 1908 mansion (tel: 401-253 2707).

December

First Night (31st), Boston, MA; Portland, ME; Burlington, Montpelier, and St Johnsbury, VT; Providence, RI; Danbury, Hartford, and Mystic, CT: Originating in Boston, First Night celebrations involve music, dance, storytelling, and performances at downtown venues, all accessible through the purchase of a single button, available at businesses in the participating cities.

Practical Information

GETTING THERE

By Air

Boston's Logan Airport (tel: 617-561 1800 or 1-800 235 6426) is the principal arrival and departure point for air travelers in New England. Regional airports include Bradley International in Windsor Locks (north of Hartford), Connecticut (tel: 860-627 3000); T. F. Green in Warwick, Rhode Island (tel: 401-737 4000); Portland, Maine (tel: 203-774 7301); Manchester, New Hampshire (tel: 603-624 6539); and Burlington, Vermont (tel: 802-863 1889). Each state also has several smaller airports, most with limited commuter service.

Visitors to southern parts of New England often choose to fly into one of the major New York City area airports – Kennedy, La Guardia, or Newark – and continue their travels via rail, bus, or rental car.

By Rail

Amtrak (1-800 USA RAIL) operates several routes serving major New England cities and points in between. Boston's South Station is the northern terminus of Amtrak's North-east Corridor, which links the city with New York City and Washington, DC via Providence and New Haven; trains – including the new high-speed, extra-fare *Acela* – operate on a frequent schedule every day. Amtrak's *Lake Shore Limited* runs daily between Boston and Chicago, with stops at Worcester and Springfield, Massachusetts. The *Vermonter* operates daily between Washington, DC and St Albans, Vermont via New York City, Hartford, Springfield, and major Vermont cities and towns. The *Ethan Allen Express* runs between New York and Rutland, Vermont.

By Bus

Greyhound (tel: 1-800 231 2222) and its regional affiliates serve major population centers and in-between points throughout New England, and link the region with its terminals in New York City, Montreal, and points south and west.

Peter Pan Bus Lines (tel: 617-426 7838 or 1-800 237 8747) also links Boston and a number of other southern New England locations with New York City.

By Car

New England is well served by the US Inter-state Highway system. I-95, the main coastal artery, connects New York City with New Haven, Providence, Boston, and Portland. East–west I-84 links southern New York State with eastern Massachusetts via Hartford. The Massachusetts Turnpike (I-90) joins the New York Thruway near Albany. North–south I-89 crosses into Vermont from Quebec southeast of Montreal, and links with Boston-bound I-93 at Concord, New Hampshire. North–south I-91 runs between New Haven and the Vermont-Quebec border.

TRAVEL ESSENTIALS

Visas and Passports

To enter the United States you must have a valid passport. Visas are required for some nationalities, and also for stays exceeding prescribed time limits. Consult the nearest US embassy or consulate in your home country for details.

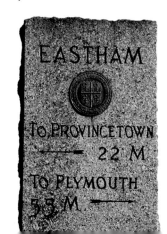

Left: snowmobiling at Warren, Vermont
Right: old town markers still abound

Customs

Anyone over the age of 21 may take into the US 200 cigarettes, 50 cigars (other than Cuban) or 3lbs (1.36kg) of tobacco; 1 US quart of alcohol; and duty-free gifts worth up to $100. You are not allowed to bring in meat products, seeds, plants, or fruits. Don't even think about bringing narcotics, and carry a current prescription, signed by your doctor, for any medications not available over the counter. The US permits you to take out anything you wish, but consult the consulate or tourist authority of the country to which you are traveling next for details of its customs regulations on entry.

Weather

New England is characterized by major seasonal variations in weather. Even within the same season, and area, the weather can be changeable. In general, coastal regions have moderately warm but breezy summers; cool, damp springs; mild falls; and damp winters marked by occasional 'Nor'easter' storms capable of bringing high tides and snow. Southerly interior regions will often be warm and humid in summer, except at higher elevations; in the north, summer weather is comfortably warm and, in the mountains, can be chilly in the evening. In the northern interior, snowfall can easily total more than 100in (2.5 meters) each winter, with some mountain regions receiving three or four times that amount. Winter weather in the southern half of the region is more moderate, with considerably less snowfall.

The famously colorful fall foliage is at its peak between mid-September and late October. The colors start earliest in the far north and at high elevations.

Clothing

In winter, pack a parka or woolen coat, gloves, warm hat, and weatherproof boots. For all other seasons, assume that you will encounter at least one cool spell, and carry a sweater or light jacket. Raingear is advisable, particularly in spring.

Like the rest of the US, New England has grown increasingly less formal over the past few years, and casual clothing will see you through most situations. However, shorts, jeans, and T-shirts are still frowned upon in many of the better restaurants, particularly in cities; and the finest Boston establishments – as well as a few traditional mountain, seaside, and lake resorts – still expect jackets (and, in a few cases, ties) for men. A neat pair of khakis together with a blazer is virtually failsafe; women should not encounter any problems with a casual dress or pantsuit.

Electricity

The United States uses 110–120V, 60-cycle AC voltage (as opposed to the 220–240V, 50-cycle of Europe). Laptops and most travel appliances are dual voltage and will work in both US and Europe but you should check first. An adaptor will be needed for US sockets: these may be purchased at airport pharmacies and department stores.

Time Zones

All of New England is on Eastern Standard Time. It is 3 hours ahead of Los Angeles, 1 hour ahead of Chicago, 5 hours behind London, and 15 hours behind Tokyo. New England is 1 hour behind the Canadian provinces of New Brunswick and Nova Scotia. (Remember that Daylight Saving Time is in effect between specified dates in early April and late October; turn clocks ahead one hour in spring, back one hour in fall.)

Business Hours

Most offices are open Mon–Fri 9am–5pm, although some open at 8am. Banks are open Mon–Fri 9am (sometimes 9.30am –3pm, often until 4 or 5 later in the week. Saturday banking hours, usually mornings only, are becoming less common.

Post offices are usually open Mon–Fri 8am–5pm, Sat 8am–noon. In Boston, the main post office at 25 Dorchester Street is

Left: apple time in New England

open 24 hours a day. Mail may be addressed to General Delivery at any post office; make sure the zip code is included in the address.

Stores are generally open from 10am (sometimes 9) till 6pm, often until 9 on Thursday and Friday and through the week in the big malls. Except in malls and popular tourist areas, shops may close on Sunday.

Money Matters

Travelers checks are the most convenient way to carry large sums, although travelers are increasingly inclined to withdraw funds from ATM machines, which are abundant throughout New England, except in the remotest rural areas. American Express and Visa travelers checks are the most widely accepted, at nearly all stores, restaurants, and hotels, but identification may be required. Credit cards (Visa, Mastercard, American Express, Discover, and Diners Club) are also widely honored, but be sure to check with waiters or clerks beforehand.

Health

Health care in the US is expensive; foreign visitors should obtain health insurance before leaving home.

Information Sources

Massachusetts: **Massachusetts Office of Travel and Tourism**, 10 Park Plaza, Suite 4510, Boston, MA 02116 (tel: 617-727 3201 or 1-800 227 6277); www.massvacation.com.

Connecticut: **Connecticut Office of Tourism**, 505 Hudson Street, Hartford, CT 06106; (tel: 1-800 282 6863); www.ctbound.org.

Rhode Island: **Rhode Island Dept of Economic Development, Tourism Division**, 1 W. Exchange St, Providence, RI 02903; (tel: 401-222 2601); www.visitrhodeisland.com.

Maine: **Maine Tourism Association**, Box 2300, 325B Water Street, Hallowell, ME 04347; (tel: 207-623 0363 or 1-888 624 6345); www.visitmaine.com.

New Hampshire: **New Hampshire Office of Travel & Tourism Development**, Box 1856, Concord, NH 03302; (tel: 603-271 2343 or 1-800 386 4664); www.visitnh.gov.

Vermont: **Vermont Chamber of Commerce**, Box 37, Montpelier, VT 05601; (tel: 802-223 3443); www.vermontchamber.com.

Phone Numbers
Emergency (Medical and Police): 911

Credit Cards (Lost or Stolen):
AmEx: 1-800 528 2121
Mastercard: 1-800 826 2181
Visa: 1-800 227 6811
Discover: 1-800 347 2683

International Dialing Codes
To dial other countries (other than Canada, which shares the US system), dial the international access code, **011**, then the country code as follows:
Australia: 61
France: 33
Germany: 49
Italy: 39
Japan: 81
Mexico: 52
Spain: 34
United Kingdom: 44

Local Dialing Codes
Area dialing codes, preceded by a 1, must be used when dialing outside a code area; in some locations, the code must be used even when calling within the area. Four states in New England have one code each:
Maine: 207
New Hampshire: 603
Rhode Island: 401
Vermont: 802

Massachusetts employs codes 617, 508, 781, 978, and 413, depending on location. All Boston phones are in area code 617; phones in the far-western part of the state are 413. Cape Cod is 508. Check all other locations in a telephone directory.
Connecticut uses codes 860 and 203; Hartford is 860, New Haven 203. Check all other locations in the directory.
Numbers beginning with area codes 800 or 888 are toll-free if dialed within the US.

Tipping
Tipping is of course voluntary, but waiters, taxi drivers, bartenders, and hairdressers will

all expect a gratuity amounting to 15 percent of the bill, or 20 percent for above-average service. On restaurant checks over $100, a 20 percent tip is the norm. Tips are not included in restaurant checks, except for big parties; when calculating, do not tip on tax.

Doormen, skycaps (airport porters), and porters receive about $1 per bag.

MEDIA

Newspapers and Magazines

The national edition of the *New York Times* and *USA Today* are both available throughout New England except in the smallest and most remote towns; while both are national newspapers, the *Times* contains the more comprehensive coverage of national and international news.

The most respected New England daily, the *Boston Globe*, is available throughout the region. The major New England cities and large towns have their own dailies which, with local and regional weeklies, are valuable sources of information on clubs, concerts, and events.

The *Phoenix* (covering Boston), *Advocate* (western Massachusetts), and *Seven Days* (northern Vermont) are just a few examples of college-area weeklies that have in-depth

coverage of local events and performances, and an alternative slant on the news.

When it comes to interesting periodicals and magazines, *Yankee* covers the region with down-home, human-interest angles, and also carries frequently essential travel features. Other publications that might prove relevant to your visit and which are worth checking out include *Vermont Life*; *Down East* (Maine); and *Boston*.

Radio and Television

Major New England cities have affiliates of the principal US TV networks – NBC, CBS, ABC, Fox, and PBS (Public Broadcasting System for cultural, news, and educational content). Cable or satellite hookups carry these and numerous other stations, including the world-renowned CNN, to the majority of hotels and motels. (Note that a lot of country inns deliberately choose not to furnish their rooms with TV sets).

Hundreds of radio stations (AM and FM) broadcast throughout the region; in general, AM stations carry more local-interest content, while the stations of *National Public Radio* (FM) carry more in-depth national news, classical music, and jazz. In northern regions, the Canadian Broadcasting System (CBC), with its excellent musical programs, can be heard clearly.

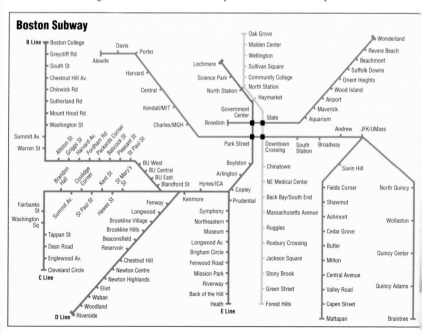

Boston Subway

GETTING AROUND

ew England is best traveled by automobile. In addition to the Interstate Highway system, the region is served by an excellent system of secondary federal and state highways, and county and municipal roads. Roads are generally well maintained, with every effort made to remove snow promptly; but in rural areas you might encounter miles of unpaved roads that can be tricky in winter or in the mud season that arrives with the spring thaw.

Road signs can cause problems even for experienced locals – you won't have trouble on major routes, but you may feel abandoned on some secondary roads. It's always a good idea to travel with detailed maps, such as the one included in the back of this guide.

The speed limit on Interstate Highways in New England is 65mph (105kph), except in urban areas where it is 55mph (90kmh). On secondary highways in rural areas, the limit is usually 50mph (80kmh). In built-up areas, you must slow to 20–40 mph (32–64kph); city speed limits rarely exceed 25mph (40kph). Look out for signs – limits can change abruptly, especially on the outskirts of towns. A right turn on a red traffic signal is permissible after a complete stop anywhere in New England, except where there's a No Turn on Red sign. At a rotary (roundabout), yield to vehicles already in it.

Nowhere in New England is city driving enjoyable, or generally necessary – but in Boston, it can be downright harrowing. If you drive into Boston, put your car in a garage and leave it there for the duration of your stay. If you plan to embark on a driving excursion of the hinterlands from the city, don't rent a car until you're ready to leave.

Car Rental

Major US car rental firms are represented at Boston's Logan Airport, as well as at smaller airports and many city locations throughout New England. Note that drivers must be 21 to rent a car in Boston, and that rental agreements may forbid taking a car rented in New England to New York or New Jersey without payment of a surcharge. Children under the age of five or under 40lbs (18kg) must be protected by a child safety seat, available at extra cost.

Compare prices from the following major rental firms:
Avis (tel: 1-800 331 1212)
Budget (tel: 1-800 527 0700)
Dollar (tel: 1-800 800-4000)
Hertz (tel: 1-800 654 3131)
National (tel: 1-800 227 7368)
Rent-A-Wreck (tel: 1-800 535 1391)
Thrifty (tel: 1-800 847 4389)

By Rail

In addition to the Amtrak routes, commuter rail transportation is provided in eastern Massachusetts and between Boston and Providence by the Massachusetts Bay Transportation Authority (MBTA). The MBTA also operates Boston's system of subways, trolleys, and elevated trains. For details of schedules and other information, call 617-222 3200 or 1-800 392 6100. One- to seven-day visitor passes are available.

By Bus

An MBTA bus service connects Boston with its suburbs and outlying cities. Other metropolitan areas in New England also have a local bus service. For intercity bus travel within the region, contact Greyhound or Peter Pan Bus Lines. Other regional carriers are Bonanza Bus Lines (tel: 1-800 556 3815), serving New York, Boston, and Cape Cod from Providence; and Plymouth and Brockton Buses (tel: 508-746 0378), linking Boston with Cape Cod and points along Massachusetts' South Shore.

Above: on the ferry to Martha's Vineyard

ACCOMMODATIONS

In New England, hotels, motels, inns, and B&Bs abound. Reservations are important when traveling in summer, in the fall foliage season, and near popular winter resort areas. Savings can be considerable at small, independent motels, albeit at some sacrifice in decor and central location.

In the following listings, approximate price categories (for a standard double room) are indicated thus:

$ = under $75
$$ = $75–$150
$$$ = $150–$200
$$$$ = Over $200

Connecticut

Griswold Inn (31 rooms)
36 Main Street, Essex 06426
Tel: 860-767 1776. Fax: 860-767 0481
www.griswoldinn.com
Many of the suites in this 1776 inn (the oldest inn in the US) have fireplaces. All rooms have private baths and period furnishings. There's a lively taproom (bar) and a restaurant that serves classic New England fare; Sunday brunch is a tradition. $$–$$$

Steamboat Inn (10 Rooms)
73 Steamboat Wharf, Mystic 06355
Tel: 860-536 8300. Fax: 860-536 9528
www.visitmystic.com/steamboat
This renovated riverfront warehouse, just steps from the historic drawbridge, is a good choice for luxurious accommodations. Big, antiques-filled rooms have been beautifully decorated and have whirlpool baths; some feature wet bars and fireplaces. $$$–$$$$

Whalers' Inn (41 rooms)
10 East Main Street, Mystic 06355
Tel: 860-536 1506 (800-243 2588 outside Connecticut). Fax: 860-572 1250
www.whalersinmystic.com
Located one block from the Mystic River, this in-town complex includes a wonderful country inn, plus a motel complete with Victorian furnishings and reproduction four-poster beds. The restaurant specializes in nouvelle Italian cuisine. $$–$$$$

Maine

The Castine Inn (20 rooms)
Main Street, PO Box 41, Castine 04421
Tel: 207-326 4365. Fax: 207-326 4570
www.castineinn.com
Opened in 1898, the gracious Castine Inn, located near the harbor, offers spacious accommodations. Guests can enjoy the sauna, a wraparound porch, and a common room with a fireplace. The restaurant specializes in seafood; also be sure to try the excellent country breakfast. $$

Kenniston Hill Inn (10 rooms)
Route 27, PO Box 125, Boothbay 04537
Tel: 207-633 2159 (800-992 2915 outside Maine). Fax: 207-633 2159
www.innkeeper@maine.com
A 200-year-old colonial inn near the town green. Large rooms with private baths and/or shower, fans, and decks: five have working fireplaces. Country breakfast is served by candlelight. $$–$$$

he Maine Stay (9 rooms)
2 High Street, Camden 04843
el: 207-236 9636. Fax: 207-236 0621
ww.mainestay.com
his 200-year-old colonial inn in the High
treet Historic District has comfortable,
ntiques-filled rooms (two with shared bath),
cozy family room, and parlor with fire-
lace. Full breakfast and afternoon tea.
ooms in the rear are quietest. $$

Mira Monte Inn (13 rooms)
9 Mt Desert Street, Bar Harbor 04609
el: 207-288 4263 (800-553 5109 outside
Maine). Fax: 207-288 3115
ww.miramonte.com
All rooms in this 1864 in-town Victorian
nn have a private bath, air-con, TV, and fire-
lace and/or balcony. The living room and
brary have fireplaces, and there are 1½ acres
f manicured grounds. Breakfast features
ome-baked breads and pastries. $$–$$$

Massachusetts
Boston/Cambridge Area
Boston Harbor Hotel (230 rooms)
70 Rowes Wharf (Financial District), Boston
Tel: 617-439 7000. Fax: 617-752 7077
www.bhh.com
Board the airport water shuttle at Logan and,
within minutes, enter this sumptuous hotel.
All rooms have harbor or skyline views, 18
are equipped for the disabled. Lap pool. Near
financial district and aquarium. $$$$

Fairmont Copley Plaza (379 rooms)
138 St James Avenue (Back Bay), Boston
Tel: 617-267 5300. Fax: 617-437 0794
www.fairmont.com
European-style *grande dame* of Boston's
hotels, although some of the rooms are on
the small side. The rooms in front look out
on Copley Plaza and Trinity Church. $$$$

Harborside Inn (54 rooms)
185 State Road (Faneuil Hall)
Tel: 617-723 7500. Fax: 617-670 2010
www.hagopianhotels.com
Set in a 19th-century warehouse, this hand-
some option features decent-sized rooms
with polished wooden floors, Oriental rugs,
and reproduction Victorian furniture. Ele-
vators, exercise room, and restaurant. $$$

Sheraton Commander (175 rooms)
16 Garden Street, Cambridge
Tel: 617-547 4800. Fax: 617-868 8322
www.sheratoncommander.com
A traditional, well-maintained property not
far from Harvard and Radcliffe Yards. A
number of rooms have kitchenettes; others
have four-poster beds. $$$

Outside Boston/Cambridge Area
Allen House (6 rooms)
18 Allen Place, Scituate 02066
www.allenhousebnb.com
Tel: 781-545 8221. Fax: 781-545 8221
Handsome home near Scituate Harbor;
recently renovated with Arts & Crafts decor.
Features garden suite with Jacuzzi and pri-
vate patio entrance, and the only ramp-access
handicapped room in the area. Full gourmet
breakfast a specialty. $$–$$$

Deerfield Inn (23 rooms)
81 Old Main Street, Deerfield 01342
Tel: 413-774 5587 or 800-926 3865
Fax: 413-775 7221
www.deerfieldinn.com
All of the rooms at this 1884 inn have period
wallpaper and furnishings: some have four-
poster or canopy beds. The common rooms
are filled with antiques. Restaurant features
a contemporary American menu. $$$

Garrison Inn (24 rooms)
11 Brown Square, Newburyport 01950
Tel: 978-499 8500. Fax: 978-499 8555
www.garrisoninn.com
Listed in the National Register of Historic
Places, this 1809 mansion has been carefully
restored: features include original brick walls
and hand-hewn wooden beams. American
menu features prime rib and lobster. $$–$$$

Hawthorne Hotel (89 rooms)
18 Washington Square, Salem 01970
Tel: 978-744 4080 or 800-729 7829.
Fax: 978-745 9842
www.hawthornehotel.com
Salem's only full-service hotel, this Federal-
style red-brick building is on the Green and
handy for all downtown attractions. The
rooms are all furnished with 18th-century
reproductions. Three restaurants, bar,
lounge, and exercise room. $$$

Left: there are plenty of upscale B&B accommodations throughout New England

Historic Merrell Inn (10 rooms)
1566 Pleasant St/Rte 102, South Lee 01260
Tel: 413-243 1794 or 800-243 1794
Fax: 413-243 2669
www.merrell-inn.com
The inn's history, which spans more than 200 years, is reflected by furnishings such as wide-board floors, a 'bird cage' colonial bar and Federal-era antiques. Several rooms have working fireplaces; all have private baths. Breakfast is cooked to order. $$–$$$

The Masthead (21 units)
31–41 Commercial St, Provincetown 02657
Tel: 508-487 0523 or 800-395 5095
Fax: 508-487 9251.
www.TheMasthead.com
Pleasant complex of shingled houses with rooms, efficiency (self-catering) apartments, and cottages. Private boardwalk, beach, and dock. $$–$$$

Moses Nickerson House (7 rooms)
364 Old Harbor Road, Chatham 02633
Tel: 508-945 5859 or 800-628 6972
Fax: 508-945 7087
www.capecodtravel.com/mosesnickerson house
All of the guest rooms in this gracious 1839 home, situated just a short walk from town, are filled with antiques, and are individually decorated. They also all have queen-size beds and private baths. $$$–$$$$

Yankee Clipper Inn (8 rooms)
96 Granite St, PO Box 2399, Rockport 01966
Tel: 978-546 3407 or 800-545 3699.
Fax: 978-546 9730
www.yankeeclipperinn.com
1929 Art Deco mansion on 1½ oceanfront acres (0.6 ha) has well-appointed and charmingly decorated guest rooms: six are oceanfront. Salt-water pool. $$$–$$$$

New Hampshire

Adair (8 rooms)
Old Littleton Road, Bethlehem 03574
Tel: 603-444-2600 or 888-444 2600
Fax: 603-444 4823.
www.adairinn.com
The area's most luxurious inn offers some of the finest dining in its restaurant, Tim-bir Alley. Guest rooms in the three-story

Georgian Revival mansion, set in 200 acre overlooking the mountains, are decorate with period antiques and reproduction some have fireplaces. $$$

AMC/Pinkham Notch Camp and Huts
Route 16, Pinkham Notch
(reservations: Box 298, Gorham 03581)
Tel: 603-466 2727
www.outdoors.org
Accommodations at the base of Mt Wash ington include bunkrooms, private, and fam ily rooms, all with shared bath. Three meal are served daily, and there's a living roo with fireplace. The AMC also maintains eigh full-service huts (meals, beds, blankets) fc hikers, and several other lodges. $

Bernerhof Inn (13 rooms)
Route 302, Box 240, Glen 03838
Tel: 603-383 9132 or 800-548 8007
Fax: 603-383 0809
www.bernerhofinn.com
Guest rooms in the inn have private bath and old-world comfort; those in the anne have Jacuzzis, air-conditioning, and TV. Th highly-acclaimed restaurant specializes i Swiss, classic French, and new America dishes. A Taste of the Mountains cooking school is headquartered here. $$

Inns at Mills Falls (101 rooms)
Routes 3 & 25, Meredith 03253
Tel: 603-279 7006 or 800-622 6455
www.millfalls.com
Three contemporary inns surround a 40-f (12-meter) waterfall: the original Mill Falls Inn; Bay Point, which is directly on the lake and The Chase House, which has fireplaces and pleasant sitting areas. The complex includes five restaurants and 18 stores. Indoor pool, sauna, and spa. $$$–$$$$

Mt Washington Hotel & Resort (200 rooms)
Route 302, Bretton Woods 03575
Tel: 603-278 1000 or 800-258 0330.
Fax: 603-278 8838
The *grande dame* of the White Mountains opened its doors in 1902. This hotel, a National Historic Landmark, offers a wide variety of accommodations, including spacious suites, and a full complement of resort activities. Rates are MAP and meals are

Right: the Mt Washington Hotel in the White Mountains'

served in the festive, formal dining room. There's also a quiet country inn on the grounds. $$$$

The Notchland Inn (12 rooms)
Route 302, Harts Location 03812
Tel: 603-374 6131 or 800-866 6131
Fax: 603-374 6168
www.notchland.com
Gustav Stickley designed the fireplaced living room of this 1862 mansion at the entrance to Crawford Notch. Each of the spacious, handsomely decorated rooms has a wood-burning fireplace and private bath: some have private decks and Jacuzzis. A five-course gourmet dinner is served in the dining room. MAP rates available. $$$–$$$$

Sise Inn (34 rooms)
40 Court Street, Portsmouth 03801
Tel: 603-433 1200 . Fax: 603-431 0200
www.someplacedifferent.com
The Sise Inn, set in a Queen Anne town house in the city's most historic district, has rooms in the main inn and in an addition built in the 1980s. All are decorated with Victorian-era furnishings and include antique reproductions, private baths, and TVs: some have whirlpool baths. $$–$$$$

Rhode Island

Atlantic Inn (21 rooms)
High Street, PO Box 188, Block Island 02807
Tel: 401-466 5883 or 800-224 7422
Fax: 401-466 5678
Located on a hill overlooking the harbor, and dating back to 1879, the Atlantic Inn features Victorian-furnished rooms, complete with private baths; some have ocean

views. The restaurant specializes in seafood and prime beef, and has an excellent wine list. Breakfast is served buffet-style. Closed Nov–Apr. $$$–$$$$

The Ivy Lodge (8 rooms)
12 Clay Street, Newport 02840
Tel: 401-849 6865
www.ivylodge.com
This Stanford White-designed Victorian 'cottage' in the mansion district features a 33ft- (10 metre-) high Gothic paneled oak entrance and a three-story turned-baluster stairway. The Ivy Lodge's guest rooms have private baths, period furnishings, brass or iron beds, and fireplaces. Hearty buffet-style breakfasts. $$–$$$

The Hotel Viking (237 rooms)
1 Bellevue Avenue, Newport
Tel: 401-847-3300 or 800-556 7126
Fax: 401-848 4864
www.hotelviking.com
This in-town National Register of Historic Places property blends historic detail with guest comforts. Rooms – particularly suites – are spacious and well-equipped. There's an indoor pool, hot tub, sauna, restaurant, and a rooftop bar. $$$–$$$$

Vermont

Basin Harbor Club (77 cottages, 38 rooms)
Basin Harbor Road, Vergennes 05491
Tel: 802-475 2311 or 800-622 4000
Fax: 802-475 6545
www.BasinHarbor.com
The family-oriented Basin Harbor Club, a lakefront cottage resort situated on some 700 acres (283 ha) and with fine views across

Lake Champlain, has been a popular resort for over 100 years. The activities on offer include an 18-hole golf course, boating on the lake, children's programs, and a health club. The restaurant serves classic American cuisine, but be warned that jackets are required at dinner. Closed mid-Oct–mid-May. AP or MAP rates available. $$$-$$$$

Green Mountain Inn (78 rooms)
Main Street, Stowe 05672
Tel: 802-253 7301 or 800-253 7302
Fax: 802-253 5096
www.greenmountaininn.com
Many of the rooms and suites at the Green Mountain Inn – which dates back to 1833 – and at the annex in the center of town feature canopy beds, a fireplace, and a Jacuzzi. All have private baths and are furnished with antique reproductions. Amenities include a swimming pool, an athletics club, and two restaurants – one with an outdoor patio. $$–$$$$

Inn at Shelburne Farms (24 rooms)
Bay and Harbor Road, Shelburne 05482
Tel: 802-985 8686. Fax: 802-985-8123
www.shelburnefarms,org
The 60-room Webb family mansion (dating to 1899) on the grounds of a working farm / National Historic Site, offers luxurious, period-decorated guest rooms (some with private bath), an excellent library, spectacular views of Lake Champlain, and some of Vermont's finest dining. Closed mid-Oct–mid-May. $$$–$$$$

The Inn at Weston (13 rooms)
Route 100, PO Box 179, Weston 05161
Tel: 802-824 6789. Fax: 802-824 3073
www.innweston.com
The original inn at this three-building complex dates to 1848. Accommodations are luxurious, with fresh-cut flowers, Ralph Lauren comforters, and Lindt chocolates. Many of the rooms have wood-burning fireplaces, whirlpool tubs for two, and TVs. Contemporary regional cuisine is served in the candlelit dining room; award-winning wine list. $$–$$$$

Lilac Inn *(9 rooms)*
53 Park Street, Brandon 05733
Tel: 802-247 5463 or 800-221 0720.
Fax: 802-247 5499
www.lilacinn.com
The emphasis is on luxury and romance at this elegant 1909 Greek Revival mansion in landscaped grounds. The second-floor guest rooms are spacious and airy, with elegant bathrooms and some fireplaces. The menu at the seasonal dining room changes often; breakfast and Sunday brunch are always superb. $$–$$$$

The Middlebury Inn (75 rooms)
14 Courthouse Square, Middlebury 05753
Tel: 802-388 4961 or 800-842 4666
Fax: 802-388 4563
www.middleburyinn.com
A historic, 1827 rambling brick inn with beautifully restored, well-appointed rooms in the main inn and the Victorian-era Porter House Mansion, as well as accommodations in the attached contemporary motel. Tea is served daily from 3 to 4pm; the restaurant serves traditional American fare. $$–$$$$

Trapp Family Lodge (193 rooms)
700 Trapp Hill Road, Stowe 05672
Tel: 802-253 8511 or 800-826 7000.
Fax: 802-253 5740
www.trappfamily.com
Established by the von Trapp family of *The Sound of Music* fame, this European-style lodge on 2,700 acres includes a motel-style building and timeshare units. Amenities include pools, kids' programs, tennis courts, a sports center, hiking trails, and three restaurants. MAP rates available. $$–$$$$

Left: the Trapp Family Lodge in Stowe

The Woodstock Inn & Resort (144 rooms)
14 The Green, Woodstock 05091
Tel: 802-457 1100 or 800-448 7900
Fax: 802-457 6699
www.woodstockinn.com
Laurence Rockefeller's flagship property offers upscale country hospitality. The lobby's stone fireplace sets the tone for the Woodstock's elegance. Spacious guest rooms have colonial furnishings; some have porches and/or fireplaces. Amenities include a fine restaurant, coffee shop, swimming pool, and privileges at the local Woodstock Country Club. $$$–$$$$

Budget Accommodations
Youth Hostels:
Hosteling International
1105 Commonwealth Avenue
Boston 02215. Tel: 617-779 0900
www.hiayh.org/home.shtml

B&B Referrals:
New England
Destinnations New England
572 Route 28, West Yarmouth, MA 02673
Tel: 800-333 4667
www.destinnations.com

Vermont
BnBFinders. Tel: 888-547 8226
www.bnbfinder.com

Vermont and Western Massachusetts
American Country Collection of B&Bs.
Tel: 800-810 4948
www.bandbreservations.com

Maine
Quaker Tavern B&B/Referral Service.
Tel: 207-797 5540

Rhode Island, Boston, and Cape Cod
B&B of Rhode Island, Inc
Tel: 800-828 0000
www.visitnewport.com/bed and breakfast

Connecticut
Bed & Breakfast Ltd. Tel: 203-469 3260
Martha's Vineyard and Nantucket Reservations (MA): Box 1322, Lagoon Pond Rd., Vineyard Haven 02568
Tel: 800-649 5671 or 508-693 6868

FURTHER READING

Reference
Insight Guide: New England (7th edition, 2001), Apa Publications. Comprehensive coverage of the whole of New England, with travel tips and stunning photographs.

Insight Guide: Boston (2nd edition, 2001), by Marcus Brooke, Apa Publications. A combination of detailed and insightful reporting on all aspects of the city, with a vivid, photo-journalistic style of illustration.

Insight Pocket Guide: Boston (3rd edition, 2000), by Marcus Brooke, Apa Publications. Essential itineraries and points of interest in and around Boston, amply illustrated with photographs, and with pull-out map.

Amory, Cleveland, *The Proper Bostonians*, Parnassus Imprints. An affectionate, witty study of Boston society that also serves as an introduction to the charms of Americana.

Beston, Henry, *The Outermost House: A Year of Life on the Great Beach of Cape Cod*, Henry Holt. A classic of naturalism that describes a year spent on a Cape Cod beach.

Thoreau, Henry David, *Walden; Or, Life in the Woods, Dover Thrift*. 19th-century philosophical treatise about man's relations with nature and society.

Whalen, Richard, *Truro: The Story of a Cape Cod Town*, Parnassus Imprints. An up-to-date account of a New England community with splendid historical photos.

Fiction
Hawthorne, Nathaniel, *The Scarlet Letter*, Library of America. Love in a Puritan community.

James, Henry, *The Bostonians*, Penguin Classics. Proto-feminist novel about high society in Boston in the 19th century.

Wharton, Edith, *Ethan Frome*, Norton. Tragic novel written in 1911 about a man trapped by his circumstances, and the complexities of modern life.

practical information

Also from Insight Guides...

Insight Guides is the classic series, providing the complete picture with expert and informative text and stunning photography. Each book is an ideal travel planner, a reliable on-the-spot companion – and a superb visual souvenir of a trip. 193 titles.

Insight Maps are designed to complement the guidebooks. They provide full mapping of major destinations, and their laminated finish gives them ease of use and durability. 100 titles.

Insight Compact Guides are handy reference books, modestly priced yet comprehensive. The text, pictures and maps are all cross-referenced, making them ideal books to consult while seeing the sights. 127 titles.

INSIGHT POCKET GUIDE TITLES

Aegean Islands
Algarve
Alsace
Amsterdam
Athens
Atlanta
Bahamas
Baja Peninsula
Bali
Bali Bird Walks
Bangkok
Barbados
Barcelona
Bavaria
Beijing
Berlin
Bermuda
Bhutan
Boston
Brisbane & the
   Gold Coast
British Columbia
Brittany
Brussels
Budapest
California,
   Northern

Canton
Cape Town
Chiang Mai
Chicago
Corfu
Corsica
Costa Blanca
Costa Brava
Costa del Sol
Costa Rica
Crete
Croatia
Denmark
Dubai
Fiji Islands
Florence
Florida
Florida Keys
French Riviera
   (Côte d'Azur)
Gran Canaria
Hawaii
Hong Kong
Hungary
Ibiza
Ireland
Ireland's Southwest

Israel
Istanbul
Jakarta
Jamaica
Kathmandu Bikes
   & Hikes
Kenya
Kraków
Kuala Lumpur
Lisbon
Loire Valley
London
Los Angeles
Macau
Madrid
Malacca
Maldives
Mallorca
Malta
Manila
Melbourne
Mexico City
Miami
Montreal
Morocco
Moscow
Munich

Nepal
New Delhi
New Orleans
New York City
New Zealand
Oslo and Bergen
Paris
Penang
Perth
Phuket
Prague
Provence
Puerto Rico
Quebec
Rhodes
Rome
Sabah
St. Petersburg
San Diego
San Francisco
Sarawak
Sardinia
Scotland
Seville, Cordoba &
   Granada
Seychelles
Sicily

Sikkim
Singapore
Southeast England
Southern Spain
Sri Lanka
Stockholm
Switzerland
Sydney
Tenerife
Thailand
Tibet
Toronto
Tunisia
Turkish Coast
Tuscany
Venice
Vienna
Vietnam
Yogjakarta
Yucatán Peninsula

ACKNOWLEDGEMENTS

Photography	
6B, 16, 37T/B, 38T, 49, 59, 71, 81, 85	**Natasha Babaian**
11	**Benson J Lossing**
34B	**Carlotta Junger**
1, 2/3, 5, 7, 8/9, 10, 20 ,21, 23T/B,	**Joanne Pearson/Fair Haven**
24T/B, 25, 28T/B, 30, 31, 32, 33, 35,	**Photographs**
38B, 39, 41T/B, 42, 43, 45T/B, 46,	
47T/B, 48T/B, 50, 51T/B, 53, 54, 55T/B,	
56T/B, 57, 58, 60, 61, 62, 63, 64, 65,	
66T/B, 67, 68, 69, 73, 75,	
78, 80,82, 86, 89, 90	
7B, 13, 15	**Topham Picturepoint**
26, 76	**Mark Read**
Cover	**Tony Stone**
Back cover	**Joanne Pearson/Fair Haven**
	Photographs
Cartography	**Berndtson & Berndtson**
Cover Design	**Tanvir Virdee**

INDEX